Jeremiah Samuel Jordan

Considerations on the causes and alarming consequences of the present war and the necessity of immediate peace

Jeremiah Samuel Jordan

Considerations on the causes and alarming consequences of the present war and the necessity of immediate peace

ISBN/EAN: 9783337226695

Printed in Europe, USA, Canada, Australia, Japan

Cover: Foto ©ninafisch / pixelio.de

More available books at **www.hansebooks.com**

CONSIDERATIONS

ON THE

CAUSES

AND

ALARMING CONSEQUENCES

OF THE

PRESENT WAR,

AND THE

NECESSITY OF IMMEDIATE

PEACE.

BY A GRADUATE OF THE UNIVERSITY OF CAMBRIDGE.

Tolerabilius effet, fi res Eorum, quorum intereft, monomachiis finiretur. Sed quid commeruere cives et agricolæ, qui fpoliantur fortunis, exiguntur fedibus, trahuntur captivi, trucidantur, ac laniantur? O ferreos principum animos, fi hæc perpendunt, ac ferunt: ô craffos, fi non intelligunt; fupinos, fi non expendunt.

ERASMUS to BERALDUS.

LONDON:

PRINTED FOR J. S. JORDAN, NO. 166, FLEET-STREET.

M DCC XCIV.

PREFACE.

⸻

THE following pages were written before the opening of the prefent Campaign. It was thought neceffary to mention this circumftance, to account for the Author's filence on fome recent facts. The Bill for raifing a Corps of Emigrants would not have paffed unnoticed, had not the Manufcript been fent to the Prefs before its introduction to the Houfe; fince it forms an important æra in the progrefs of the war, and muft confequently be interefting to all claffes of Readers. The Author might have been accufed of mifreprefentation by Ariftocratic Readers, if any fuch look into this Pamphlet, in defcribing the affairs of France in fo flourifhing a ftate, after the late difpatches from the Duke of York, if the period at which

he wrote had not reconciled the feeming incongruity : his filence on the meditated fubfidy
for Pruffia might have offended the friends of
Reform, had it not been evident that he
wanted opportunity to animadvert on the
meafure as it deferved. It will not be improper
to fay a few words on each of thefe fubjects.

Had the Author conceived that any fubfequent events had in the leaft degree invalidated
the force of his arguments, he would have
fuppreffed the publication : but being convinced that every new tranfaction only confirms
the neceffity of a change in our politics, he
fubmits his " Confiderations" with deference to
thofe, who intereft themfelves in fuch fpecu-
lations.

With regard to the King of Pruffia's fecef-
fion, and fubfequent demands, they fully fhew
that the fufpicions of his fincerity, expreffed
in the firft chapter of this work, were well
founded ; and may operate as a warning to our
credulous Adminiftration, not to place impli-

cit

cit confidence in the royal affurances of their other Allies. That fuch exorbitant demands are likely to be complied with by a Britifh Parliament, affords an occafion for fuch re-flections, as it would not be prudent in an Author to fuggeft.

At the clofe of the laft Campaign, the French were making rapid incurfions into Germany; of which notice has been taken in the fecond chapter: the Combined Armies are at this time advancing into France, and the trium-phant ftyle of our late Gazettes may by fome be thought to refute thofe arguments, founded on the military prowefs of our Antagonifts. But there is no foundation for fuch an opinion. As the Campaign advances, the hopes and fears of either party will be alternately agitated by the viciffitudes of war; uninterrupted fuccefs is feldom the lot of an invading army; and where the courage and conduct of the invaded is ac-knowledged, we know not how foon the aggref-fors may be compelled to retrace their fteps, and renounce their hopes of conqueft for the fafety

of

of retreat. Nor would this affertion be invalidated, if the Combined Armies were within twenty miles of Paris: fhould they ever penetrate far into the enemy's country, let them beware of the fate of the Duke of Brunfwick, and remember that to retire is often attended with more difficulty than to advance.

In the mean time, though the forces of the Allied Powers have effected a footing in the French territory, we do not find the predictions of Minifters verified: the late accounts from the Continent do not inform us, that the inhabitants flock to the ftandard of Royalty, or receive with any fymptoms of gratitude thefe forcible Champions of their interefts.

The Emigrant corps has been hinted at towards the conclufion of the fourth chapter; a fhort obfervation will be fufficient for it here. A meafure more replete with cruelty, more embarraffing or more expenfive was never adopted; it carries the termination of the war,

as

as far as depends on the movers of it, to an infinite diftance; it unveils the real defigns of Adminiftration, and expofes the hypocrify of their pretexts: the war is now acknowledged to be for the reftoration of Defpotifm and Ariftocracy.

The following pages were partly written, with the hope of impreffing fome minds with a more juft idea of our prefent fituation. The Author has not fo inordinate a fhare of vanity, nor is he fo entirely unacquainted with the political world, as to imagine that any fuggeftions will gain the attention of Statefmen, which proceed from an obfcure writer, unfupported by party: but being convinced that multitudes of private perfons fupport Adminiftration in their different capacities, only becaufe they are not accuftomed to think on the fubject of government, he wifhes to lead fuch perfons to inveftigate the conduct of their public fervants, and to awaken in them a fenfe of their duty as Members of the Community. But a confiderable inducement to

the

the Author to publifh his fentiments at this time, was that he might affert the privilege of an individual, in imminent danger in thefe days of profecution : the privilege of declaring opinions adverfe to the ruling powers, and of canvaffing with freedom the public meafures of public men.

May 1, 1794.

CON-

CONSIDERATIONS, &c.

CHAPTER I.

ON THE SITUATION AND RESOURCES OF ENGLAND.

WHEN men are engaged in any project, prudence points out the following confiderations to their notice. Their firft concern will be, to form an exact eftimate of the powers, which themfelves poffefs for the accomplifhment of their purpofes : their fecond, to inquire into the obftacles which rivals may interpofe for the counteraction of their defigns ; to which the laft and moft important fucceeds ; from a comparifon of the force employed on either fide, and the balance of probabilities, to determine on their courfe of action ; to perfevere with fpirit in confidence of merited fuccefs, or defift with prudence from confcioufnefs of inferiority.

Much

Much is it to be regretted, that this rational procedure fhould have been deemed unneceffary, by thofe who prefide in the Councils of this Nation : believing that the voice of warning may yet be heard with advantage, that the path to which reafon directs is not yet irrecoverable, I would ftrenuoufly infift on the neceffity of attending to the foregoing confiderations.

Let us enter upon the difcuffion of the firft article : let us confider the circumftances in which we ftand; the powers which are allotted us, to attain the end propofed. Now in the performance of this office, it will become us not to imitate the conduct of certain Statefmen in Office, who reprefent every occurrence in the moft flattering point of view; but to enter on the fubject with manlinefs and a fpirit of improvement; to examine the unfavourable fide of the queftion with feverity, that we may obviate its difficulties; and to appreciate the talent we poffefs with fcrupulous exactnefs, that we may not overftep the boundaries of moderation.

But before I enter on the difcuffion of my fubject, let me enter my caveat againft thofe
miftakes

miftakes or mifreprefentations, to which authors of my particular fentiments are conftantly expofed : let the tendency of the following pages be thoroughly underftood ; to
inftitute an inquiry, whether the prefent meafures of the King's Minifters will promote the
real interefts of the country ; or whether dif-
férent principles of conduct may not be neceffary to avert thofe national calamities, prog-
nofticated by the inaufpicious foothfayers of
the Oppofition.   But here the cautious writer
ftops ; he ventures not in the prefent crifis to
fuggeft the poffibility of imperfection in a fyftem, which enables the Servants of the Crown
to influence, if not control, the Reprefentatives of the Nation ; he allows himfelf not to
imagine that the welfare of the community,
either in the prefent or in any poffible ftate of
affairs, cannot be fecured without a radical
Reform ; he accedes without examination to
the favorite pofition of the day, that the
Houfe of Commons were never intended to
reprefent the people at large : fhould it even
be further infifted, that the people at large never ought to be reprefented, he will compliment the fupporters of thefe opinions with a
carte-blanche upon the fubject : into perilous
difquifitions concerning the Britifh Conftitution,

tion, he is not prepared to plunge : he con-
fesses himself profane ; unworthy to be initiated into the facred myfteries of Government : he entertains an adequate fenfe of the
bleffings he undefervingly enjoys ; and fub-
fcribes with deference to the propriety of certain profecutions, and the delicacy with which
the facred privileges, freedom of fpeech, and
the liberty of the prefs, have been treated in
the late equitable and humane fentences. Influenced by fentiments like thefe, he fears not
to incur any unfavorable imputation from the
admirers of the prefent men and meafures, if
he endeavours to turn their attention to fubjects, on which they do not appear to have
thought, and to recommend a mode of proceeding to which they do not feem at prefent
to be favorably inclined.

The fteps which I mean to purfue, I have
before enumerated ; and, apologizing for this
explanatory digreffion, I fhall proceed to inveftigate the real fituation of this country,
and the powers with which it is invefted. And
here I muft premife, that as far as an offenfive
war againft France is concerned, the picture I
fhall draw, will be that of imbecility, not of
ftrength : I fhall be obliged to fubftitute impo-

tence

tence for power, and fhall have occafion to fpeak of burdens more frequently than of re-fources. It might be deemed prefumptuous in an unknown writer to enter fo freely into fub-jects of this nature, which have engaged the attention of the firft literary characters, did not the complexion of the age plead in his juf-tification. But political inquiries are become fuch general topics of ftudy, not folely to the ftatefman, the fcholar, or the fpeculative re-clufe, but to mankind at large in the profef-fional, the mercantile, even the laborious claf-fes, that any man of common fenfe, who has read or thought on fuch matters with earneft-nefs, may communicate the opinions he has formed, unawed by the imputation of te-merity.

The embarraffments, occafioned to this country by the American war, are too feelingly remembered by the public to need recapitula-tion : the privation of territory in which that unhappy conteft ended, is by this time gene-rally acknowledged to have been a blcffing ; but the addition of a hundred millions to our debt has eclipfed the brighteft glories of Great-Britain ; has difabled her from arrefting the Defpots of the Continent in their carcer of

conqueft, and forbidden her poets and hiflo-
rians any longer to hail her the Patronefs of
Liberty, or the Champion of the Human race.
Declamation and argument were unremit-
tingly employed to deprecate the impofition
of burdens fo fevere : the acceffion of fix
millions annually to the ftanding taxes, not
inconfiderable before, excited in the breaft of
the people the mingled emotions of diffa-
tisfaction and defpondency ; the public difcontent alarmed the Adminiftration of the
country ; and a change of fyftem was re-
luctantly adopted, becaufe deftruction feemed
to impend over the profecution of hoftilities.
Thus was the American, like all ambitious
wars, marked with calamity in its progrefs,
and difgrace in its conclufion. But the lenient
hand of peace adminiftered timely relief to
the diforders of the political conftitution, and
the profperity by which its abode with us was
accompanied, exceeded the hopes of the moft
fanguine. In fuch a fituation, when the return
of reafon might enable us to repair the vio-
lences committed in the hour of infanity,
fhould we not have perfifted in availing ourfelves of the bleffed opportunity? That we
ought to unite with heart and hand for the
prolongation of tranquillity ; to direct the
energy

energy of the national character to the improvement of our manufactures and the ex-
tenfion of our commerce, the proper fources
of our political confequence ; to atone for paft
extravagance by the future economy of our
eftablifhment ; was repeatedly and ftrenuoufly
enforced by the ableft Statefmen, the moft
fenfible writers, and the moft enlightened philofophers of the time. By a fyftem like this,
and by the diligent cultivation of thofe liberal
and philanthropic principles, on which the fa-
bric of our conftitution is faid to have been
erected, it would have been within our grafp
to have been the foremoft, among the nations
of Europe, in the caufe of patriotifm, virtue,
and univerfal benevolence. This was the
theatre worthy of our exertions ; on this ftage
our powers would have been difplayed with
advantage ; but in the fanguinary tragedy at
prefent exhibited to the world, the lot of Great-
Britain is caft among the inferior characters of
the dramatis perfonæ ; like the meffenger of
the ancient drama, fhe is faddled with the un-
thankful office of developing the plot ; while
the heroes and demigods of Germany and
Pruffia are entrapping the applaufe of the
fpectators, by the lofty fentiments, with which
they glofs the felfifhnefs of their defigns.

When

When the prefent Minifter came into office, he was thought, by fome of his partizans, to have been fent from Heaven : and to prove the divinity of his miffion, he profeffed to enter upon the great work of Redemption : the plans of the ableft financiers were collected, and their merits affumed by the great Law-giver and Prophet; Dr. Price* favored him with three unacknowledged communications, and the leaft efficient of the three was adopted. This however was the epoch at which our Salvation is faid to have commenced : the profperity of the nation was gradually to be regenerated, and the praifes of the country's guardian angel were reiterated from one end of the ifland to the other. There were in-deed who thought, that the means were inade-quate to the end ; that the ftatements were fal-lacioufly reprefented ; and that his object with regard to the people was their amufement more than their benefit. How far thefe ob-jections were founded, I am not competent to judge; but there were others who thought (and among their numbers I am happy to

* I have derived my information on this fubject from the Doctor's relation and friend, Mr. Morgan; who in a pamphlet of a few pages has by a plain tale completely put down the Minifter.

mention

mention Mr. Burke, whofe mind the French
Revolution had not then palfied) that
exertions of a different nature muft co-
operate with the preceding, before the intended effect could be produced. Prudence
in the management of our foreign and domeftic concerns; the reformation of abufes, the re-
duction of idle retainers on our different eftablifhments, and the fecurity of independence
to the Houfe of Commons, were meafures which
it was not then deemed fedition to recommend.

Thefe doctrines the fon of Chatham had at
his entrance into life embraced and taught;
and it was expected, that what he had fo liberally promifed while in the minority, he
would have attempted to perform when in office. But how inconfiftent with himfelf is the
fame man, when from being the advocate of the
people, he is tranflated to the fervice of the
Crown! Thofe enviable improvements for which
the Patriot labours, are innovations dangerous
to the Minifter; right and wrong, liberty and
flavery alter their natures, as he changes his
place; and methods lefs detrimental to himfelf muft be found, or the welfare of fociety
muft be abandoned. Thus were the afpiring
hopes of thofe, who called themfelves the

C   friends

friends of Reform, extinguiſhed: but the
proſpect, though diſtant, of relief from burden, ſupported and animated the ſpirits of the
public: few were competent to criticize the
means propoſed; all were ſolicitous for the
fulfilment of the end. In this ſituation of affairs, the tranquillity of the country, the ſpi-
rited exertions of commercial men, and the
rapidity of improvement obſervable among
the people, the effect of peace, and of its probable continuance, were attributed by Courtiers and Paraſites to the projects of the Miniſter. But even he, when expatiating on his
ſucceſs at each ſucceeding Convention of Parliament, uniformly confeſſed, that the accom-
pliſhment of his intention, depended on the
permanence of tranquillity, and the conſe-
quent vigour of public credit. Nor could the
moſt obſtinate aſſertor of our national ſuperiority, flatter himſelf with the maintenance of
that ſuperiority, if with ſuch a complication of
debts already incurred, and with ſuch increaſed
expences even on our peace eſtabliſhment, we
were to be implicated ſo ſpeedily in another
war; which muſt not only overturn the Miniſter's theory of Finance, but reduce him again
to the practice of taxation. But it will be a
neceſſary ſtep in this inveſtigation, to examine
the

· the grounds on which we are committed, the cauſe in which our powers are to be exerted. That the debt of the country was enormous; that the taxes which muſt be levied annually for the payment of its intereſt, and for the current expences of the Executive Government, preſſed moſt ſeverely on the induſtrious poor, even during a time of peace; the experience of every man will certify: and from hence I have drawn a fair concluſion, that nothing but the moſt inevitable neceſſity ſhould have induced us to have plunged deeper into the ocean of difficulty, or to have again braved the torrent, which had before ſo nearly overwhelmed us. This reaſoning has been ſeduluously applied, when it happened to be in uniſon with the wiſhes of Adminiſtration. Why did Great-Britain, ſo forward in arrogating to herſelf the limitation of conqueſt, continue a ſilent ſpectator at the ſcandalous diſmemberment of Poland? Why were not the ſubſcriptions of individuals rendered effective by the interference of Government? Becauſe the ſituation of our Finances rendered it unadviſable for us to mediate between the Continental Powers: becauſe prudence muſt ſupplant generoſity; becauſe our domeſtic proſperity muſt not be ſacrificed to the intereſts of humanity. Oh that this frigid

gid caution, which arrefted us from fuccouring
a caufe fo noble, had not been difdained, when
we were committed to the fupport of Ariftocracy! When the rights of an independent nation were ufurped by foreign invaders, policy
induced us to remain inactive fpectators; but
no fooner have the French afferted their independence, by eftablifhing a Republic, than all
the fuggeftions of œconomy are forgotten; the
burdens impofed by former wars are to be
augmented, reafons for difcontent to be renewed, pecuniary difficulties enhanced, we
know not to what extent, while dangers, of
which the mention is too awful to be hazarded,
may refult from the conduct we purfue. And
to what end are we voluntarily relinquifhing
our brighter profpects? To combat a fhadow, terrific in appearance; but whofe cor-
poreal exiftence has never been verified; to
avert a mifchief whofe nature is undefined, and
whofe operation has never been afcertained by
experience: to exterminate the fpirit of liberty
from among a people, left the dæmon of li-
centioufnefs fhould contaminate its purity: in
fhort, we have been fo eager to range ourfelves
under the banner of royalty, that we have deferted from the ftandard of humanity.

But

But we mult not leave unrefuted the affertions of the Alarmifls : they call the prefent a
war of felf-defence ; and talk of the wanton
and unprovoked aggreffion of France, without
which we had ftill remained, both at home
and abroad, in the enjoyment of the bleffings
of peace. Partial and uncandid reprefenta-
tion !—founded on fiftion and unfupported by
evidence. The following turn is given to the
ftory. The French, in the end of the year
1792, had formed a daring projeft ; which
aimed at nothing lefs than the diffolution of
our government ; and in this laudable purpofe, they were to be abetted by a party here,
who had already founded the trumpet of fedition. What were the intentions of this formidable band, we have been in a great meafure left to conjefture : but from the horror
which they infpired; fufpicion cannot ftop fhort
of an embrio confpiracy, by which our graci-
ous Monarch was to be dethroned ; a bloody
anarchy erefted on the ruins of order and
proteftion, and our infular independence an-
nihilated by an unnatural union with France.
Thus was the tocfin founded, by which the
good people of England were terrified into
acquiefcence in Mr. Pitt's meafures ; nay, multitudes were fo befide themfelves as to rejoice

in

in the hoftile determinations of the Britifh
Cabinet. But Minifters knew in their confciences, that confpiracies in the metropolis,
and invafions from the continent were the off-
fpring of their own prolific brain, or the fa-
brications of their dependents, for the double
purpofe of interefting the paffions of the multitude, and affaffinating the reputation of the
patriotic focieties. Both in the Houfe of Commons, and elfewhere, perfons in office, who
muft, if any, have intelligence of fuch illegal
proceedings, have been repeatedly challenged
to produce inftances of difaffeétion : but they
have uniformly hurried from faéts to declamation ; and though lavifh in general inveétive,
have been incompetent to the accufation of individuals. They recolleét with regret that
themfelves, improvidently as it has turned out,
together with the moft enlightened members of
the community, have long fince expreffed a
defire, that an amendment in the Adminiftration of public affairs might be effeéted; they
have direéted the minds and converfation of
men to this fubjeét ; and multifarious have been
the opinions and theories of the literary and
political world. In all this there was no great
harm ; but they have ftimulated in the people
at large, even in the lower claffes, an appetite

for

for information ; they have opened their eyes
to the perception of reafon ; and now, when
it is too late, they endeavour by alarm to ftifle
the fenfations they have awakened ; to preci-
pitate the adult man into fecond childhood.
But though confiderable has been the alteration which the minds of the people have undergone, there never has been, as I firmly believe, any fyftem, at home or abroad, by which
the government of this country was to be fub-
verted, or either of its conftituent parts abo-
lifhed ; no affemblies have been held, but, according to the phrafe in vogue, upon con-
ftitutional grounds ; the popular focieties, fo
univerfal throughout the kingdom, have not
merited the epithets with which they have
been branded ; nor has the delufion hitherto
been generally fuccefsful, by which patriotifm
was to be confounded with treafon.

But it is well known, that the cry of danger in the State was merely a pretext : to thofe
who wifh to difcover the true reafon for this
clamour, by which the feelings of popular indignation have been artfully excited, we need
only point out the difcuffions and controver-
fies, which originated with Mr. Burke, and
which were gradually directing the attention

of

of the public to the neceffity of a fubftantial Reform. To fupprefs opinions, fatal to the perpetuation of abufes, though aufpicious to the reftoration of order and happinefs, was the objeft for which the Affociations of Penfioners were formed. In the beginning of the French Revolution, Mr. Burke, relying on the prowefs, with which he was wont to wield his pen in the caufe of Liberty, thought proper, for reafons beft known to himfelf, to defert to the ftandard of Ariftocracy. But he went from the ftronger to the weaker party; his former Allies were converted into powerful Antagonifts; nor could the warmth of his defcriptions or the brilliancy of his imagination withftand the conviction, which the found fenfe and cogent arguments of his competitors forced upon the minds of the people. It was hoped that his eloquence would have prejudiced his admiring countrymen againft the incipient exertions of the French: but when experience on the contrary proved, that the rough, but energetic appeals of Paine interefted men's paffions in the fuccefs of their augmented ftruggles, a new fyftem of policy was to be adopted; the ebullitions of honeft zeal were to be reftrained by the timidity of prudence; freedom of opinion was to be

curbed

curbed by apprehenfions of political infe-
curity ; and two mighty powers were to be
precipitated into enmity, left the reafon of this
nation fhould control the ambition of its Governors.

Thefe I, in my confcience, believe to have
been the private motives for the war ; but an
opportunity occurred, which partly relieved
Adminiftration from the odium attendant on
fuch a meafure : France anticipated our declaration ; and exulting in the intemperance
of her fpirit, Mr. Pitt repulfed the attacks of
the Oppofition by pleading the want of an alternative. The jealous forwardnefs of France
was indeed unfortunate ; fince it gave a temporary popularity to the war in this country,
which all the artifices of the Alarmifts were
not able to excite. And yet if we examine
into circumftances, the conduct of the French
will not furnifh the juftification of Miniflers :
it would be idle, it would be impudent to
· deny, that hoftilities were determined here
previoufly to the aggreffion of our neigh-
bours : it muft further be admitted, that our
intentions were manifeft to them ; and that
the confequences, whether good or ill, are of
our own feeking, and reft upon our own
D   heads.

heads. It is well known by thofe, who have vifited France fince the Revolution, and whofe refidence in the country, enabled them to judge with certainty of the public temper, that hoftile defigns againft England formed no feature in their Politics; on the contrary, the Convention, as a mirror in which the countenance of the people was reflected, and the people themfelves deprecated a war with that ifland, which they were defirous to confider as the cradle of liberty: peace with England, faid they, and we challenge the continent of Europe; we thirft for the blood of defpotic Kings, of Ariftocratic Generals, and fervile armies; but let Britannia watch the combat at a diftance, arbitrate between the combatants, and beftow her fmile of approbation on the victories of virtue and humanity. Such were the fentiments which the writer of thefe pages was accuftomed to hear at every table d'hôte which he frequented, when at Paris in the fummer of 1791. Such would ftill have been the prevailing fentiments, had not the movers of our government deviated from the direct path of plain dealing into the obliquities of ftate policy. But when they faw the inclinations of the Britifh Cabinet pointing towards hoftilities, when they

3   •   obferved

obferved the anxiety with which they courted opportunities for purfuing thofe inclinations, the enthufiafm of their admiration was diminifhed : when the communications of their Ambaffador began to be difregarded by our court ; when he was treated with perfonal coldnefs and difdain, the fervour of their friendfhip for us was likely to abate : when this right of modelling their own government began to be called in queftion, refentment fucceeded to the fpirit of fraternity, and precipitated them into declarations of defiance. But can it be denied that their conduct was the confequence of ours? Did not we " marfhal them the way that they fhould go ?" They did not adopt the alternative of war, till they had reafon to think that peace was incompatible with independence : they cultivated our alliance, while we fuffered them to find a value in our intercourfe : but the fentiment fo common in private life, they found applicable to national concerns ; when affection has ceafed, acquaintance becomes hateful. Thus was the favorable opportunity neglected, when we might have formed an union of interefts with France on terms the moft honourable to ourfelves, by which we might have eftablifhed and preferved

the

the general tranquillity, and arrested the progrefs of defpotic ambition in the North. A
project worthy the liberality of Englifhmen!
A project fruftrated by that mercenary and
ambitious fpirit, that influences the general
conduct of political leaders, and prevents
them from acting on thofe extenfive principles of public good, which if adopted
would render them the patrons, but when
deferted the tyrants of their fpecies.

But the fulfilment of our treaties required,
that we fhould protect Holland from invafion: was this to be effected by no other
method, but by making ourfelves parties in
the quarrel? Are we certain that amicable
remonftrance — that impartial arbitration,
would not have met with better fuccefs, in
inducing the Republic to relinquifh their
views of conqueft, than has attended on the
operations of the laft campaign? But this ex-
periment was not tried: our imperious Allies
required our affiftance in arms, not in negotiation: they expected us to ftifle, not to
cherifh, the nafcent Commonwealth. Thefe
treaties indeed, with the folemnity of which
the advifers of peace have continually been
filenced, feem not altogether fuited to the
genius

genius of Great-Britain. An ifland, feparated
from the continent by the decree of nature ;
by the peculiarity of its fituation, and by
the difpofition of its inhabitants, marked
out for the emporium of commerce; by its
political conftitution furnifhed with fome
portion of democracy, can derive but little
benefit from an intimate connexion with
ftates, linked together in a complicated chain
of alliances, deriving their confequence from
the purfuit of military achievements, and
eftablifhed on the principles of arbitrary government and the divine right of Kings.
But however thefe engagements are to be lamented, they have been formed; Parliament
has fan&tioned them, and the people muft, I
fuppofe, acquiefce in the determination of
their rulers. I would only fuggeft to the
higher powers, to ftop fhort in time; and
not to abide by thefe vaunted treaties and
conventions to the ruin of this country : I
only intimate, that auguft as they are, they muft
give way to the care of our domeftic interefts, and the prefervation of internal tranquillity.

To return to the argument founded on the
obfervance of our engagements.—I have
already

already flated, that no attempt was made, to
fecure the independence of Holland and the
Netherlands by negotiation : but I fhall go
further, and remind my countrymen, that
the invafion of thefe territories was the pretext, not the caufe of our hoftile preparations. The conquefls of the French were aftonifhing in their rapidity ; the days of their
profperity were brilliant, but the period of
their adverfity had been long : but a few
weeks before they over-ran the Netherlands,
inftead of the befiegers, they were the befieged : the armies of Auftria and Pruffia
were in the heart of France, far advanced
on their march to the metropolis : and yet in
that important crifis, the afpect of our government was threatening, though its fword
was not drawn: the Dutch were in no
danger, when the Duke of Brunfwick was
rioting in the vineyards of Champaigne : on
the principle which we now find it con-
venient to profefs, that of maintaining the
much boafted, but little regarded balance
of power, the French, as placed in the
lighter fcale, were then entitled to our pre-
ponderating influence : but our interference
on that fide of the queftion would have mi-
litated againft the fyftem on which we really
proceeded.

proceeded. To fum up this part of my fubjeƈt as briefly as poffible, the following is pretty generally known to be the truth: From the moment that the French by the mouth of their reprefentatives conftituted themfelves a Republic, the meafures of this country were determined; their execution was only delayed, till an oftenfible reafon, more confonant with the equity of the nation than the real, could be devifed. The fub-fequent fuccefies of Dumourier prefented a favorable occafion, and the proteƈtion of our Allies gave colour to a proceeding, which originated in enmity towards Gallic Repub-licanifm, and in a refolution not to return to the original principles of the Britifh Con-ftitution. Difference of opinion upon the propriety of a war has been faid to have exifted among the Members of the Cabinet: the Premier has been exonerated from the imputation of finifter motives, and credited for his wifhes to perpetuate peace; but fuch apologies are of little avail: men aƈting in concert participate the praife of blame at-tached to the refult of their deliberations; and in this cafe it was fufficiently evident, that the predominant opinion was, that free-dom of inquiry was to be filenced by alarm

at

at home, and freedom of action was to be
destroyed by the point of the bayonet
abroad : the diffentients, if fuch there were,
who facrificed their fentiments to their fitu-
ations, merited the fevereft reprobation of
every liberal mind. But the views of the
Minifterial Party were ftill further promoted,
by the execution of Louis the Sixteenth.
The eloquence of Parliamentary Orators was
all called forth, to work upon the compaffionate feelings of the multitude, and ftimulate them to revenge this outrage upon
loyalty : the character of that unfortunate
man was extolled, the mildnefs of his difpofition, and the feverity of his fufferings defcribed in the moft pathetic terms; that nothing might be wanting to reconcile the
people to a war, fo evidently detrimental
to their interefts. I am not the perfon to
exult in the mifery of a fellow-creature, or
to depreciate the generous difpofitions of my
countrymen : nor am I fufficiently acquainted
with the merits of the cafe, to determine on
the propriety of the punifhment inflicted:
but however atrocious may have been the
conduct of the tribunal by which Louis was
condemned, I have no difficulty in afferting,
that the injurious treatment of an individual
by

by a foreign nation, whatever his rank or
fituation, can afford to us no juft occafion
for the commencement of hoftilities: nor
have I much approbation to beftow on that
fpecies of humanity, which fhudders with
horror at the decapitation of a Monarch,
while it calmly devotes thoufands of the
plebeian order to perifh by the fword. But
is it poffible that the good people of England fhould have been deceived? Treaties
are trifles light as air, when incompatible
with the prefent purpofes of Statefmen;
when acceffary to their views, they acquire
confirmation, ftrong as Holy Writ. The
Allies, whofe interefts are at this moment
dearer than our own, we have formerly been
accuftomed to watch with the eagle-eye of
jealoufy. The King, whofe misfortunes we
fo paffionately commiferate, was one of the
inftruments by which the fceptre of America
was wrefted from our gripe: nor have Kings
or Minifters been celebrated for that difinterefted generofity, which can abforb the
ranklings of difappointment in the emotions
of fraternal piety, when the object of that
piety has no remuneration in his power.

E . Thefe

Thefe obfervations lead us to the difcovery of the truth; the prefent is a war againft opinions; its objeft is to fix the colour of the cameleon; to fhew Mr. Burke that the days of chivalry are not ended; that adventures as romantic as thofe of La Mancha's Knight are to be purfued, at an expence of blood and treafure, which bids defiance to calculation. The methods by which the nation has been cajoled into confent, have been alreaded pointed out: by exciting prejudices in our minds againft the innovations of the French, and apprehenfions for our domeftic fecurity. But it is fruitlefs to regret the decifions of the paft; it is for us to devife means of extricating ourfelves from difficulties, and averting the evil confequences of our fituation.

To effeft this is the aim of thefe remarks: the fteps by which I am to proceed, feem calculated to lead to conclufions moft favorable to our welfare; and to this end, even admitting the rationality of the grounds on which we firft engaged in the war, I am fimply to compare the refources we can command for its continuance, with the means of oppofition poffeffed by our anta-

3   gonifts:

gonifts : and the refult of thefe inquiries muft determine, whether the beft peace we can obtain, unattended with ignominy, fhould not be fought, in preference to perfeverance in fo unprofitable a conteft. It has been afferted in thefe pages, and the truth of the propofition is evident to every man's under-ftanding, that circumftanced as this country has been fince the clofe of the American war, nothing but the extreme neceffity of felf-defence (to fpeak politically as well as morally) could juftify the renewal of war-like preparations. It is a fundamental prin-ciple, which reafon and experience have concurred to eftablifh, that a ftate deeply in-volved in debt, of which the fubjects labour under an accumulation of taxes for the payment of intereft, is in a condition ill-for-tified againft the perils of war ; that it feldom conducts its operations with energy, or fupports its hardfhips with equanimity ; and that prudence would dictate the earlieft poffible reftoration of peace, by which only it can repair the damages, occafioned by former prodigality. This country is in the fituation above defcribed : to this country, therefore, peace is the firft and moft important object. In this place I cannot forbear contributing

tributing the teſtimony of my approbation
to the Letter of Jaſper Wilſon to Mr. Pitt ;
and muſt recommend to thoſe of my Readers who have not ſeen it, if there are any
ſuch, to loſe no time in the peruſal of a
performance, which will do much towards
inſtructing them in the true intereſts of Great-
Britain, and ſhaking the blind confidence
which they may poſſibly place in the integrity and abilities of the Miniſter.

When to the argument deduced from the
ſtate of our Finances, we add another equally
cogent, which the commercial ſpirit of the
country furniſhes in favour of a pacific ſyſtem, the inſanity of voluntarily deviating
from that ſyſtem appears in the moſt ſtriking
colours. When in conſequence of the con-
fuſion, in which the claſhing views of different
parties had involved the nations on the
continent, the trade of Europe was border-
ing on a ſtate of ſtagnation ; this more for-
tunate iſland was in a great meaſure exempt
from the calamities experienced by the contending powers, and nearly engroſſed thoſe
branches of commerce, which ſurvived the
violence of the political hurricane. It almoſt
ſeemed, as if the diſtraction of our neigh-
bours

bours was deftined to be the promotion of our own profperity: fince Europe in general, but France in particular, too intent upon the ftudy of attack and defence, to fupply her own neceffities by the induftry of her own hands, afforded unparalleled encouragement to the exertion of ingenuity in our Manufacturers: and the articles of clothing, and of military weapons at this warlike conjuncture fo conftantly in requeft, conftituted a plentiful fource of employment and fubfiftence to a very numerous branch of the community. But the benefits arifing from our neutrality were of fhort duration: England had no fooner acceded to the confederacy, than the interruption of trade, which before was partial, became general; confidence was exchanged for diftruft in all mercantile tranfactions, credit was wounded to an alarming degree, and bankruptcies, of which the extent and magnitude are unparalleled in the annals of the country, demonftrated too feelingly the deftructive confequences of the part we had taken.

The unavoidable hardfhips and diftreffes of the poor, arifing from a variety of caufes, is alfo a circumftance which places no trivial

trivial impediment in the way of our fuccefs. Such was the preffure of burdens
before the war, which operated not only
in a direct manner, but indirectly, in occa-
fioning the increafed prices of all provifions
and neceffaries; and fo little was the advance on the price of labour proportioned
to the advance on articles of fubfiftence,
that when there was employment fufficient
for the induftrious poor in our Manufac-
tories, they ftill were poffeffed of but fcanty
means for the education and maintenance
of numerous families: animal food was an
indulgence even then confined to particular
occafions in the houfes of the poor; while
thoufands of them were debarred from ever
experiencing the enjoyment of fo falutary
a means of nutrition. To thofe who are defirous of inquiring into the nature of the
grievances, under which the poor of England labour, it is with pleafure that I recommend a late publication of Mr. G. Dyer,
in which he ftates a variety of interefling
facts, and refers his readers to the moft refpectable authority; exercifing the powers of
his mind moft diligently in the invention
of remedies for the evils, which his humanity
leads him deeply to lament. This is a fubject
deferving

deferving the moft ferious confideration ; fince
the point in which I conceive our powers
for the conduct of the war to be principally deficient, even admitting its grounds
to be juft, is the means of fupporting the
laborious claffes of the community during a
feafon, in which they muft neceffarily experience the double difadvantages, arifing
from the failure of employment, and the
fcarcity of articles neceffary to a comfort-
able fubfiftence. Severe muft be the lot of
the lower orders, when the large fums collected by the tax called the Poor's-Rate are
infufficient to relieve their neceffities : and
yet, whether it be owing to mifmanagement
or other caufes, what a comparatively fmall
portion of exifting calamity does it reach !
Endlefs are the fupplies of fpontaneous charity which are devoured by the mouth of
hunger, while the cravings of appetite ftill
remain unfatisfied ! How often has it been
faid of this great metropolis, that its benevolent inftitutions are the foul of its exiftence ! The number of its inhabitants, who
become penfioners on the bounty of the public, fo far exceeds computation, and the
provifions eftablifhed by the legiflature ; that
all the exertions of public charity and private
benevolence

benevolence are fcarcely capable of fupply-ing the deficiency, and diffipating the con-gregated clouds, which have for fome time impended over the political world.

The foregoing obfervations apply to the condition of the poor before the commence-ment of the war; during its progrefs our news-papers have teemed with advertifements, and our ftreets fwarmed with paupers, ap-pealing to the humanity of the public, and imploring relief for the miferies which the madnefs of the times has occafioned. Never did any preceding year witnefs fuch fre-quent and urgent calls on the wealthy part of the community; a remedy for poverty which can be but temporary and ineffectual: while the manufacturing towns in the coun-try have exhibited fcenes of diftrefs, which the humane muft feelingly compaffionate, though the votaries of ambition and can-didates for civil offices may attempt to pal-liate their feverity, or juftify their neceffity. But if it be true, that fuch has long been the general ftate of the great mafs, and that new circumftances of difcouragement are daily arifing, which the occafional affiftance of individuals is totally infufficient to obviate ;

to

to what do we devote the moſt numerous and moſt induſtrious, conſequently
the moſt important branch of the community, when we countenance the continuance
of hoſtilities, by ſupporting the preſent perſons in power?*

The hope in which many firſt lent their influence to the meaſures of Adminiſtration,
that the buſineſs in diſpute would ſoon be
ſettled, is now extinct: no one affects to
diſbelieve, that the conteſt will, if not re-
linquiſhed on our part, be protracted and

---

* While on the ſubject of the diſproportion between the
means and the neceſſities of the poor, I ſhall quote a remarkable paſſage from the pamphlet of M. Mallet du Pan;
as it ſtrongly enforces the juſtice of my argument:

" L'inegalité toujours croiſſante des fortunes et les gaſpil-
lages d'un luxe immodéré, contraſtoient de plus en plus
avec les haillons d'une miſere laborieuſe. Par des tables de
proportion que le Comité du Commerce et des colonies a fait
dreſſer en Angleterre, ſur les réſultats de pluſieurs années, il
eſt prouvé que, dans cet iſle dont l'ivreſſe Commerciale et l'o-
pulence tournent tous les cabinets depuis trente ans, la claſſe
immenſe des gens vivant de leur travail, et leurs familles,
s'appauvriſſent, chaque jour, par la diſproportion des ſalaires
avec les ſubſiſtances." And yet we have the temerity to augment this dangerous diſproportion.

F   deſperate.

defperate. With this confideration in view,
let us look to the alteration which a few
months, a fingle campaign have effected in
the profpects of this nation: nor can any
ftronger teftimony be adduced to the importance of peace, than the comparifon of
our fituation in a commercial point of view,
at the clofe of the years 1792 and 1793.
In the year 1792, we were at peace at home
and abroad; while the continent was agitated
with the contentions of Kings and the tur-
bulence of domeftic faction. The beneficial
confequences to this ifland were apparent:
nine years of tranquillity had infpired our
manufacturers with that vigour of induftry,
and our traders with that fpirit of enterprize, which feemed to promife a new æra
of profperity in the annals of the country;
when mercantile genius fhould rife fuperior
to the fhackles impofed by the projectors
of former wars: the people rejoiced in the
hope that they were acquainted with the extent
of their burdens, and refolved to meet the
exigency of the times with fortitude and activity. When fuch were the brightning
profpects of the nation, it fhould have been
the earneft endeavour of its rulers, to re-
alize the flattering hope: neglect of fo fair

an

an opportunity would probably be fatal;
the event has juftified the prophecy. If to
the perfevering exertions of our merchants
we owed the profperous ftate of the revenue,
and the improving refources of the country; was it not evident that any event which
fhould confine the aberrations of their traf-
fic, or diminifh the public confidence in their
refponfibility, would overthrow the edifice
which hope had erected, and poifon the foun-
tain from whence we were to derive our future
happinefs and ftability ?

I have dwelt fufficiently on the agreeable
circumftances of 1792. What a contraft did
the following year prefent! A period of brilliant profperity was immediately followed by
an epoch of unexampled diftrefs and difgrace: the city of London feemed to ftand
aghaft with confternation: where will thefe
misfortunes end? was the general queftion:
in general bankruptcy, was the anfwer of
defpondency: commercial houfes which had
ftood the brunt of a century in fame and
credit, were unequal to refift this fudden
fhock: every gazette was occupied with a
long, black catalogue of misfortune; and the
merchants of the metropolis were befieged

by

by commiffions of bankruptcy, long before
the frontiers of the enemy were affailed by
the boafted valour of our armies. Prefent
deftruction was accurately proportioned to
paft profperity; had the commercial concerns of the nation been in a languid ftate
before the rupture, they might have furvived
it with comparatively little inconvenience :
but the Minifters of the day ought to have
known, or to have confidered, that commerce, fo diffufed as ours had lately been,
could ill fuftain a violent and abrupt reftraint; that the manufacturing intereft required a large demand, to defray the expences of hazardous fpeculation : that to
check that demand by a political quarrel
with their beft cuftomers, was almoft to
fign the death-warrant of the unfortunate
adventurers; that their ability to bear up
under the preffure of exifting burdens depended on induftry exerting itfelf under the
aufpices of peace : in fhort, that never was
there a period in our hiftory when we were
fo unprepared for war; when we had fo little
to gain by it, or fo much to fear from it.
Our fears were warranted by the reality : fo
rapid was the progrefs of ruin, that the interference of Parliament was neceffary to ftop

its

its career: expedients were adopted, which staggered the resolution of the more confiderate Ministerialists : for however beneficial may have been their effects, their application was unprecedented ; and the neceffity, which urged them, difcreditable to the refponfibility of a commercial nation. The dread of univerfal ruin has fubfided : but what do exifting circumftances afford in the way of confolation? The advertifements of the Committee for the relief of the weavers in Spital-Fields, though honorable to the benevolent intentions of their Authors, afford room for ferious reflection, in the mind of every thinking man. The induftrious poor are faid to be the ftrength, the very vitals of an Empire ; upon their contribution principally depends the folvency of the ftate : a large body of thofe induftrious poor, I fpeak it from the authority of that Committee, are deftitute of employment, and in a fituation little fhort of famine; fo far from being able to contribute their mite, that their entire dependence is on the fpontaneous bounty of their compaffionate fellow-citizens. Here then is one remarkable inftance, that as the exigencies of government increafe, the ability of the people to furnifh thofe exigencies is

deplorably

deplorably diminifhed. But the columns of
our news-papers are occupied with further
calls on the charity of the opulent : our Manufacturers in all parts of the country have
been driven to the defperate refource, of
enlifting as foldiers or failors; they have left
their wives and children, by this time perhaps their widows and orphans, unprotected
and deflitute : hence the eflablifhment of
funds for the fupport of thefe victims to
the myflerious machinations of flate policy.
So wide indeed have the calamities attendant on war already fpread, that multitudes
of Mechanics have been obliged to exchange
the independence of induftry for the nig-
gardly pittance of a parifh, or the precarious liberality of private donations. When
we reflect on the comparative circumflances
of two confecutive years, what are we to
expect from the protraction of hoftilities
with which we are threatened ?

The alarming evils already defcribed have
been but the natural confequences of war in
its commencement : they have originated fimply in the circumflance of our having exchanged one condition, that of peace, for
another : they have taken place before the
nation

nation has been required to exert itself for
the support of the new measures; before a sin-
gle tax for the services of the year has been
imposed, merely from anticipation of future
unavoidable embarrassments: if such be the
outset of the business, can we hope that
our situation will be bettered, when the new
burdens, which the expences of a war esta-
blishment render indispensable, shall fall on
the shoulders of the people? We have been
told from high authority, that the necessity
of additional burdens is the subject of la-
mentation to a certain distinguished per-
sonage: the grief of that patriotic bosom is
not however totally comfortless: a principal
source of its consolation is, "the complete
success of the measure which was last year
adopted, for removing the embarrassments
affecting commercial credit."* Consolation
s the forerunner of hope and confidence:
and the Representatives of the nation are ad-
vised to provide for the exigencies of the
State "in such a manner, as to avoid any
pressure which may be severely felt by the
people."

* Vide the opening of the present Session, 1794.

I fear

I fear that the united ingenuity of the whole Legiflative Body will fcarcely difcover the means of complying with the foregoing requifition : I fee more occafion to lament the neceffity of providing for commercial difficulties, than to boaſt of the fuccefs attending the provifion. The progrefs of bankruptcies may have been arreſted, but the vigor of trade and manufactures has not been renewed : the patient has been refcued from inſtantaneous diffolution, but the power of Medicine has been proved infufficient to reſtore his ſhattered frame to convalefcènce. In fuch a ſtate of the political conſtitution, can it be fuppofed that frefh impofitions will not produce frefh difficulties ? Can it be poffible, that almoſt a million of new taxes ſhould be fupported with little inconvenience by a people, already feverely preffed by the weight of former taxation ? But much praife has been beſtowed on the method by which the Miniſter has provided the fupplies of the year : the new objects of taxation are faid to be fuch, as will affect that clafs of the community who are beſt capable of augmenting their contributions. There is in my opinion much to be faid againſt the tax on paper, and on Attornies : but as I reſt my argument on
different

different grounds, I will wave the difcuffion of
this fubjeċt; and admit with the friends of
Mr. Pitt, that he has in this refpeċt done the
beft which the circumftances of the times
would allow: but having admitted the propriety of the new taxes, I do not accede to
the propofition, " that the additional preffure
will not be feverely felt by the people."

The temporary taxes for the Spanifh Arma-
ment are continued; and by this manœuvre
the Minifter hoped to overcome his difficulties; and efcape the odium which muft have
attached itfelf to him and his Party, had they
been obliged to devife new expedients for
raifing the whole fum required. But his rea-
fonings on that fubjeċt were fallacious: that
the tranfition from peace to war muft be accompanied with an increafe of expenditure,
is an axiom beyond the reach of controverfy:
that the mafs of individuals muft ultimately
make good that increafe of expenditure, is
equally incontrovertible: confequently in whatever way the bufinefs may be managed, as the
produce of former impofts is pretty accurately
appropriated, the reality of the cafe muft be,
that after all their tricks and devices, the feverity of the preffure on the fhoulders of the

· G

people

people is exactly proportioned to the amount of the levies demanded. But the fcheme of continuing expiring taxes, inftead of impofing new, was intended to delude the nation with an opinion of our refources : it was contended · that the circumftance of the temporary taxes having been endured for four years, was a proof that it was within the compafs of our ftrength to endure them ftill longer : and thus were we eafily relieved from a confiderable part of the difficulty attending the fupplies of the prefent year. This was the fubftance of Mr. Pitt's argument on opening the Budget : need its grofs fallacy be expofed ? Not all the palliating, not all the impofing eloquence of the Minifter can prevent the people from feeling a fevere difappointment ; that burdens, the feverity of which was alleviated at the time by the confideration of their tranfitory nature, and application to a particular purpofe, and by exprefs covenant to no other, are entailed on them and their pofterity : that the relief, which was folemnly promifed to the fufferers at an appointed, not far diftant period, is now poftponed ad infinitum.

In the permanent eſtabliſhment of theſe temporary taxes, a formal compact between the Government and the Nation has been infringed ; a proceeding not to be warranted by the purſuit of ambitious projects, and phantoms of ſtate policy. With ſuch cauſes of complaint in the interruption of trade, the advancing price of neceſſaries, the addition and prolongation of heavy taxes, principally to be defrayed by the middle and lower claſſes, I do not ſee that we can reckon on the poſſeſſion of reſources, to ſupport the lengthened duration of hoſtilities. In the laſt ſeſſion of Parliament, it was frequently urged as a palliation of the dreary proſpect on which we had entered, that from the magnitude of the combination the diſpute muſt ſpeedily be terminated. This ſeemed at the time to be the argument of convenience, rather than of conviction : there appeared a probability even then that the conteſt would be protracted ; and that probability is now almoſt converted into certainty, unleſs the Allies would conſent to moderate the peremptorineſs of their demands. And allowing, in compliment to the ſanguine diſpoſition of Miniſterial partizans, that no ſerious conſequences will be felt

from

from the expences already incurred, where
will be the provision for the exigencies of
futurity ? Twelve months have already
elapfed, during which we have been in
arms : immenfe fums have been expended ;
and the objeƈ of purfuit, the eftablifhment
of what is called a regular government in
France, is further from our reach than at
the outfet : the unavoidable expences of military operations have been augmented by
loffes and difappointments, infeparable from
a ftate of warfare : our advantages as members of the confederacy, certainly have not
over-balanced our difafters : events of late
have been peculiarly infelicitous : to what
do we look forward? The next campaign
may not enrich our records with more brilliant trophies than the laft : the viƈtories
we anticipate may affimilate themfelves too
nearly to the defeats we have fuftained : but
amidft all the changes and chances, attendant on the profecution of war, the only thing
certain is expence : that is equally the confequence of fuccefs and difappointment ; and
fhould the advantages of future campaigns
prove inadequate to their coft and hazard,
who can prefume on the compliance of the
public difpofition, or expeƈ the nation to

3   diveft

divest themselves piecemeal of every indulgence, for the support of obstinacy or the
gratification of ambition? That our resources
will enable us to persist but a short time,
there is no danger in affirming; that our
opponents are as nearly exhausted as ourselves, we are by no means certain; and yet
we determine to prolong the contest to the
utmost, and adhere to the determinations
we adopted in the commencement; thus re-
ducing ourselves to the alternative of abso-
lutely conquering our adversaries, or igno-
miniously retracting our assertion, that we
would on no terms be induced to treat with
the present rulers of France.

Let us now turn our attention to the military force of the Kingdom; in speaking of
which, it would be unpardonable not to notice a subject of rejoicing, which the friends
of Administration have had the ingenuity
to discover. The number of recruits for the
service of the Army the last year has exceeded the number raised in any former
year by ten thousand; and this they say is
a ground of exaltation, and betokens the
fertility of our military resources, and the
probability of our success. That it is a very
                                        considerable

confiderable augmentation of our army, I
allow: but that we have any reafon to be
overjoyed at fuch augmentation, I cannot
agree, when I reflect on the caufes in which
that augmentation has originated. I fuppofe their idea is of this kind: that while
the Army is fupplied with recruits from the
manufacturing towns, the towns, unable to
fupport the ufual number of hands in confequence of the general ftagnation, transfer
their fupernumeraries to a new employment: and thus reciprocal benefits are exchanged. In truth, our ranks have been
pretty copioufly replenifhed from the fami-
fhed band of artificers: at firft they muft
have fuffered from inexperience in the exercife of their new occupation; and I fear
they muft have found it a fervice of fome-
what more danger than that to which they
were accuftomed: cutting throats may be a
gentleman-like purfuit, but is ill adapted to
the temper of men, who are in the habit of
cultivating the vulgar arts of peace; and
fatally have thoufands experienced, that they
have only exchanged the lingerings of want,
for the more fpeedy deftruction awaiting
them in the battle. Nor is there any danger at prefent, that thofe who prefer the
chance

chance of a cannon-ball to the apprehenfion of famine, will not be indulged in their
election; frefh food for powder is continually required; and Weavers will " fill a
pit as well as better men."

But to return from Falftaff's way of thinking to my own, I cannot fee our Manufacturers and Artifans, our men of induftry
and ingenuity, who once were thought to
conftitute the ftrength and glory of the
country, feeking refuge from idlenefs and
want by carrying a mufquet, without en-
tertaining ftrong fears that the beft days of
old England are paffed; that its fenfes are
finking into dotage, that the principles of
decay are undermining its conftitution, and
preying on its very vitals. But however
eafy commercial adverfity may render it
for a time, to replace the loffes fuftained
in our engagements, it is certain that we
are a people not naturally military; a circumftance which renders it very doubtful,
whether we can long rival our antagonifts
in prodigality of human life. The devotion
of the French to the caufe in which they
are engaged, has urged them to exertions
unparalleled in the annals of mankind : but

our

our common foldiers have no fuch lively intereft in the event of the conteft : they can
have but an imperfect idea of the grounds
on which they are acting ; of the object for
which they are contending. They are told
indeed that they are fighting for their King
and Country ; and attachment to his Royal
Mafter is fuppofed to be a neceffary ingre-
dient in the compofition of a Soldier: but
it may be difficult for wifer heads than his
to comprehend, in what refpect the true interefts of either the King or the Country
can be promoted, by forcing a particular
form of government on a people, to whom
that form is odious, and who are determined to refift to the utmoft this confpiracy againft their independence. The zeal
of thefe plain, unenlightened men will be
but languid in a caufe, enveloped in a cloud
of myftery ; a caufe in which they are not
perfonally concerned ; in which valour is
exerted, and death braved, not for the pro-
tection of their families and friends, but for
a flender diurnal pittance, hardly fufficient
for their own fupport: in which the facrifice of their lives, inftead of forming a bul-
wark round their fellow - citizens, deprives
childhood of parental folicitude, and tears
from

from the hand of dependent helpleffnefs the ſtaff on which it reſted, without affording a fingle circumſtance of confolation as an equi-valent for the loſs.

Intereſted writers and fpeakers have endea-voured to prove, from the alacrity with which men have enliſted, the cordiality of their at-tachment to the caufe. But a more natural reaſon for this alacrity has been affigned; the want of employment at home ; to which may be added, the unufual liberality of the bounties which have been offered.* There is however fufficient reaſon to believe, that the ardour of young heroes is already damped by the fe-verity, with which their countrymen have been handled on the Continent; and that the reprefentations of the wounded, who have been fent home, will deter the fons of peace from fo dangerous a purſuit as that of honour, till compelled by the calls of

---

* An inſtance is known, in one regiment, where twenty guineas, a filver watch, and half a crown have been given for each man; which, after the payment of crimps, &c. will bring the total expence to twenty-five guineas per man.

hunger.

hunger. Are thefe refources too in danger
of failing? If fo, where will be the laurels,
with which paternal partiality is fo eager
to encircle the brows of an elevated
perfonage? The military hiftory of Great-
Britain will reeeive but little additional luf-
tre, when the tranfactions of the laft year
fhall have been added to its page : the glories and fplendid fucceffes, which have been
announced by Minifters in Parliament, are
of too refined and tranfcendent a nature, to
be difcerned by the dull optics of common
obfervers: the light in which paft events
have generally been viewed is unfavourable;
and reafoning of the future from the paft, we
have no caufe for exultation in the profpect
of the enfuing campaign. But we depend
with confidence on our Allies; in their mul-
titudinous armies the paucity of our numbers will be fheltered; while their vigour-
ous exertions and unrelenting difcipline will
enfure a due proportion in the honours of
victory to every member of the confederacy.

By fuch delufive hopes do we feek to
qualify the acerbity of difappointment; but
on what foundation do we build this dependence

pendence on our Allies? I fear their difficulties are greater than our own: fame is more treacherous than ufual, if the coffers of the Continental powers are not drained to the very dregs; have we not reafon to believe that the Emperor is recurring to the moft defperate expedients, to fupport the growing expences of the war? What reliance can we place on the ability of the Pruffian Monarch to co-operate with us, when he has declared his intention only to furnifh his contingent, unlefs the difburfements of his immenfe army fhall be defrayed by thofe, who he is now pleafed to fay are more interefted in the event than himfelf? What opinion can we form of his integrity, when we have experienced his conduct from the beginning to be made up of intrigue and diffimulation, when he has been willing to fulfil his own engagements, fo far only as they have been conducive to private purpofes of intereft and ambition; when his demands have been uniformly exorbitant, and his fervices frequently fallen far fhort of reafonable expectation?— Such are the parties with whom we have pledged ourfelves to act in concert; on whom we truft for the execution of important conditions. To complete the catalogue of our

expenfive

expenfive follies, and augment the unavoidable burdens of a war, we have affented to a modeft requeft; that of fubfidizing our Allies, for the defence of their own territory, and the prefervation of their own interefts. So great is the importance of the conteft in which we are engaged, fo liberal the fpirit with which we difdain the fuggeftions of prudence and œconomy! In fhort, when we confider the difadvantage, under which we entered upon a fyftem of hoftilities; the events, civil and military, which have occurred during its progrefs; the prefent circumftances of ourfelves and our Allies, and the diftance at which we are placed from the fcene of action, a circumftance favorable in fome points of view, but difadvantageous in others; we can hardly flatter ourfelves that futurity has any compenfation in ftore for us, adequate to our hazard; or that our defperate exertions will end in the attainment of our object, indemnification for the paft and fecurity for the future.

CHAP.

C H A P. II.

ON THE SITUATION AND RESOURCES OF
FRANCE.

THE next object to which it will be
necessary for us to turn our attention,
is the character and circumstances of our
opponents, and the obstacles which their
exertions may give us reason to expect.

The French nation have for centuries at-
tracted the notice and admiration of Europe ;
they are known to be a brave, ardent, and
generous people ; fond to enthusiasm of military pursuits ; jealous of honour, and im-
patient of control. They have suffered for
ages under the oppression of arbitrary government : the Monarch exercising uncon-
trolled authority over the highest and proudest
of his Nobles ; and they in their turn insult-
ing the Bourgeois, and trampling on their
vassals. But this system, infamous as it was,
could never entirely eradicate those senti-
ments of honour and generosity which seem

to

to have been moſt bountifully imparted to this extraordinary people. There has ever been remarked among the French nobility, though equally obſequious to their Sovereign, and tenacious of their own privileges, a ſenſibility and rationality in their pride, a dignity and a courteſy even in their inſolence, which is not commonly diſcoverable in the frequenters of a Court : while thoſe in a lower ſphere of life, though degraded by ſervitude, and abjectly devoted to the caprices of their ſuperiors, were neverthelefs diſtinguiſhed by a pleaſing levity of manners, and an amiable kindneſs and hoſpitality to ſtrangers, which rendered their metropolis the favorite reſort of European travellers, and contributed to veil the defects of their moral and political character.

But though their conduct under the former ſyſtem was marked with theſe inconſiſtencies, the new character, which they have lately aſſumed as Republicans, ſeems not to be ſufficiently underſtood. To account for the ſeeming incongruity of this change, will be a neceſſary preliminary to the diſcuſſion of my ſubject.

It

It has frequently been mentioned as matter of furprife, that the fentiments and difpofitions of fo populous a community fhould have undergone a complete metamorphofis in fo fhort a fpace of time : that the ftrain of panegyric, which refounded with the praifes of the Monarch and the bleffings of his reign, fhould have inftantaneoufly modulated into fongs of popular triumph, and epithalamiums of liberty : nay more, that the overwhelming enthufiafm of the Parifian populace fhould have fpread immediate contagion through fo extenfive a territory ; and that the inhabitants of Provinces, remote from each other and from the Capital, fhould with one heart and one voice have affented to an order of things, all the poffible effects of which were not as yet to be calculated or forefeen. But though the French Revolution be aftonifhing in its origin and progrefs ; it is not fo much to be admired for the fuddennefs of its introduction, as thofe who are unacquainted with the previous ftate of that country may fuppofe. Literature and philofophy had for years been gradually extending their influence over France : the writings of the moft eminent advocates in the caufe of liberty, both ancient and mo-

dern,

dern, Greek, Roman, and Englifh, were familiar to men of rank and education; and
that the unlettered multitude might not be
debarred from thofe celeftial irradiations,
which illuminated the minds of their fuperiors, their writers tranfplanted the Republican
fpirit of paft ages into their own works,
and blended the dignified fentiments of the
ancient Grecians, with the wit and vivacity
of modern Frenchmen.

And here I cannot but admire the pro-
vidential impolicy of the old Monarchy,
which deviated from the principle of fimilar
eftablifhments; which aimed at uniting the
permanence of Defpotifm with the advance-
ment of knowledge. We know that under
the other arbitrary governments of the world,
the acquifition of learning is far from being
encouraged; unlefs it be of that abftrufe
and merely theoretical kind, of which there
is no danger that the multitude fhould be
enamoured: nay, rational ideas of religion
among the people are fo far deprecated in
Catholic countries, that the fervice of the
church is ordained to be performed in a
language unintelligible to the mafs of wor-
fhippers. But an affectation of refinement
and

and genius led many of the Kings and great men in France, to become the patrons of fcience: nor did royal penetration perceive the danger, that a fpirit of freedom, that lurking ferpent, might lie concealed and cherifhed under the flowers of adulation.

Louis the XIVth, that extraneous compound of imbecility and celebrity, was moft remarkably the dupe of his own vanity : the work of undermining defpotifm was begun in his reign ; towards which he was led unintentionally to contribute. This Monarch, not content with the parafitical homage of Courtiers and Sycophants, determined to extend his fame beyond the narrow precinĉts of Verfailles, by engaging the pen of genius and learning in his fervice ; and to tranfmit the memory of his reign to pofterity, as the æra of an Auguftan age.— Infatuated with this paffion for literary honours, he colleĉted round his throne the moft celebrated of Poets and Philofophers ; countenanced the labours of the famed French Academy with his proteĉtion, and in the purfuit of perfonal glory, fhook to its foundation the authority of his fucceffors, by contributing to diffipate the cloud of ignorance,

I   in

in which that authority was feated. But
this conduct proceeded, not from greatnefs
of defign, but ignorance of the confequences:
the elegant phrafeology, in which they clothed
their compliments, was grateful to the ear of
royalty; the terms in which they magnified
the uninterrupted victories, the political faga-
city, or the literary attainments of the Grand
Monarque, were not the lefs acceptable for
being unfounded in reality: nor can we tell
which moft to admire, when we look into
the Dedications, or the Academic Difcourfes
of the Day, in the Prince the credulous
avidity, or in the Authors the unblufhing
prodigality, of adulation. Satiated with the
extravagance of dedi atory compliment, he
paffed unnoticed thofe fcintillations of liberal fentiment, difperfed through the publications of the age, which occafionally fparkle
through the cloud of fervility, and betray the
genuine feelings of the enlightened mind.
There is one trait in the character of the times,
which will be acknowledged by thofe who
are verfed in the productions of the great
tragic poets, Corneille and Racine: at a period when both the theory of divine right,
and the practice of the arbitrary fyftem appeared to be in the zenith of their glory

in

in France, the theatrical pieces of thefe authors, reprefented with the fuffrage of univerfal approbation before popular audiences,
thofe particularly whofe fubject was taken
from ancient hiftory or fable, were not un-
frequently diftinguifhed by paffages of a de-
mocratic tendency, which would fcarcely pafs
the ordeal of the prefent Chamberlain's cri-
ticifm, in this more favoured age and country.

Thefe little incidental fallies made an im-
perceptible, but, permanent impreffion on the
public mind: confidence was gradually em-
boldened by impunity, and the advances of
free inquiry were fhrouded under the covering of allegiance and attachment, till the
political Argus was completely hoodwinked;
the difcipline of defpotifm carelefsly relaxed,
and the ftrong holds of tyranny at laft at-
tacked and carried by the affault of popular
enthufiafm. To this conclufion Voltaire and
Rouffeau, improving on the imperfect pat-
tern of their predeceffors, did not a little
contribute: their attempts, more bold and
methodical, though ftill under the guidance
of caution, and often under the difguife of
allegory, were more effectual: till by degrees
the force of argument and the poignancy of

3   fatire

fatire produced that fecret revolution in men's minds, which in due time openly burſt forth in their actions. But among the writers who have contributed towards this important change, I muſt direct the particular attention of the Reader to Montefquieu;* a man whoſe literary and philoſophical attainments procured him the reverence of Europe; whoſe patriotiſm, employing the powers of his mind to that nobleſt of purpoſes, the public good, excited the gratitude by promoting the rational improvement of his countrymen. To him it was referved to impreſs upon the minds of Frenchmen that ſacred truth, that every part of the ſtate ought to be equally ſubject to the laws; to inſtruct them in that principle of nature and of equity, which obliges every citizen equally to contribute his proportion, towards the happineſs of the whole, in ſhort, to digeſt the principles of liberty and law into a regular ſyſtem.

* The prophetic opinion of a cotemporary is remarkable; it is expreſſed in a note on one of Montefquieu's letters to M. Solar. " Lorſque M. de Solar en lu la premiere fois *l'Efprit des Loix*, il dit, voila une livre qui operera une révolution dans les efprits en France."—Duodec. Edit. vol. vii. Note on Montefquieu's Letter to Solar.

Such

Such was the progrefs of an event, fo eminently diftinguifhed among the memorabilia of
hiftory : an event which affords an awful
warning to the potentates of the earth, not to
attempt the unnatural union of flavery and
civilization; not to indulge the impracticable
hope, of being recorded in hiftory as the be-
nefactors, while they are in perfon the oppref-
fors of mankind. In the interval between, if
I may be allowed to adopt fuch a diftinction,
the mental and the actual revolution, when the
inclination was ripened, but the opportunity
wanting; though all was tranquil in appearance, and the ufual courfe of things continued,
difcerning fpectators could diftinguifh the
fubterranean ftorm, the eruption of which was
to overthrow with its violence the deep-laid
foundation of the monarchical eftablifhment.
The fame undiftinguifhing attachment to the
perfon of the Monarch, the fame veneration
for the ceremonies of the Church, which cha-
racterized paft generations of Frenchmen, was
profeffed during the reign of Louis XVI. in
public affemblies and promifcuous company :
but during the latter years of his fovereignty,
his fubjects became licentious in the extreme
in their animadverfions on his character, where
the familiar intercourfe of private fociety re-
moved

moved the fhackles of reftraint : there the
gluttony of the King and the gallantries of his
Confort were the unexhaufted topics of con-
temptuous ridicule : there the notorious vices of
the Prieſthood were humorouſly contraſted with
the folemnity of their funſtion ; till the fubſtance had nearly been confounded with the
ſhadow of religion : there the penury of the
Finances and the prodigality of the Court were
canvaſſed and fatirized with more than Republican feverity. In this difordered ſtate was
France for fome time previous to the Revolution : the face and figure remained fair and
graceful to the eye ; but difeafe and corruption
preyed upon its vitals. At length the critical
period either of diſſolution or renovation arrived : the ſhock was fuſtained with unex-
peſted fortitude and compofure, and the new
regimen, to which the body politic was fub-
jeſted, feemed likely to reſtore vigour to the
ſtate, and aſſiſt the operation of Reform.

This event has been compared by many
fpeculatiſts to a Meteor darting through the
ſky ; filling the beholders with aſtoniſhment
and fear at its momentary appearance, and il-
luminating the horizon with preternatural, but
temporary radiance : and in conformity with
this

this idea, they are waiting for its equally pre-
cipitate evanefcence, when the twilight of
evening fhall refume its fober reign among
the habitations of men. But were I to hazard
a conjecture concerning futurity, I fhould liken
it to the dawn of the morning, which an-
nounces the approach of the rifing fun; that
luminary, which fheds a clear, a fteady, and a
beneficial radiance over the works of nature;
which often is obfcured by temporary clouds,
and counteracted in its benign influence by the
violence of paffing tempefts: which in its
progrefs towards its meridian, can be impeded
by no power in the univerfe, but will pafs in
regular fucceffion through all the gradations
of its glory, till it arrives at the limit of its
courfe, and finks, with all the objects on which
its rays have been reflected, into the darknefs
of primeval night. Such will probably be
found to be the progreffion of rational improvement and univerfal liberty, as yet in the
imperfect and defencelefs ftate of infancy: but
which, notwithftanding all the difafters which
it has encountered, and is ftill liable to fuftain,
will gain ftrength with maturity, and correct-
nefs with experience; will obtain a firm eftablifhment in all the political fyftems of mankind,
and though delayed in its advances to fupremacy,

premacy, will retain and augment its influence and authority, as long as the world shall endure.

By these extended views were many of the first movers of the Revolution animated : but they were found unequal to the performance of what they had judiciously planned ; so that when the first excesses of joy for the demolition of the King's Fortress (as Mr. Burke has delicately called the Bastille) and for the emancipation of the country, had subsided ; and the work of forming a Constitution, more difficult than that of overthrowing Despotism, was to be commenced ; the prospect of happiness was overshadowed by the approach of tempests : it was then discovered by the intrigues and party-animosities of the National Assembly, and the influence of the corruption, which royalty found means to exercise, even in the state of impotency to which it was reduced; that permanent order and tranquillity, the end to which the insurrection was directed, was further from attainment, than the vivacity of hope would at first permit the people to believe.

It would be needless to detail circumstances already well known : for which reason I shall

pass

pafs over the frequent diffenfions which the intereft and ambition of political leaders oc-cafioned; the ftruggles between the remnant of the Court-Party, and the candidates for popular favour; and the jealoufy which the incongruities of the new Conftitution generated between the Legiflative and Executive Go-vernment: evils which led to continual tumults and difturbances, during the four years of li-mited monarchy. I have before mentioned the cordial difpofition of the French towards this country, as it appeared in 1791, which made a temporary refidence among that hof-pitable people not more interefting to the curiofity, than gratifying to the national pre-judices of Englifhmen. I can further affirm from obfervation, that Republican principles, even at fo late a period of the Revolution, and when the King's recent flight to Varennes had juftly rendered him fufpeĉted, were neither general nor popular among the citizens : and that a man who at a much frequented table d'hôte at Orleans was one day arguing in favour of a change in the form of government, appeared to me to be received by the company with almoft as much contempt and averfion, as the abettor of a fimilar fcheme would at this time excite in a Minifterial club in England.

K   This,

This, together with the determined refusal of
such a proposition in the National Assembly,
which, in the midst of the indignation excited
by the Royal treachery, was propounded but
by a few individuals, and abandoned by general
consent; proves that the adoption of Repub-
licanism was not the result of a settled plan
from the commencement of the Revolution,
but grew out of the circumstances of the
times, and the inveterate opposition of principle, which was continually widening the
breach between the Court and the people.
The demonstrations of joy and the proofs of
unanimity, which succeeded the King's accept-
ance of the Constitution, flattered the hopes of
peaceful citizens : but the purposes to which
the prerogative was imprudently applied, and
the clandestine intelligence between Louis and
his foreign connections, with the impertinent
interference of neighbouring powers in matters
of domestic concern, threw the kingdom into a
state of convulsion, which foreboded the utmost
horrors of civil contention. At length, the
multiplied instances of treachery on the part
of the Royal Family and their partizans, the
unwarranted menaces and the hostile move-
ments of the Emperor ; the desire of the
citizens to reap the harvest of their toils, by
establishing

eftablifhing a government over which they
fhould have a real, as well as nominal influence,
paved the way for a fecond Revolution, more
powerful in its effects, and more important in its
confequences than the firft.*

Having curforily reviewed the tranfactions
of the Revolution, it will be proper to notice
the change which has been produced in the
national character. The review which has
been taken of their manners and difpofitions
antecedent to thefe great events, has demonftrated the poffeffion of inherent virtue,
clouded and obfcured by the vices of government : the luxury of a Court had engendered habits of frivolity ; the morals of a
Court had encouraged inconftancy and infin-
cerity : the prepofterous inequalities of condition had overwhelmed the fenfe of natural
independence, and habituated the mind to the
exactions of ufurped fuperiority. But in the
courfe of the late ftruggles, difficulties and
hardfhips have reftored the enfeebled energies

* The meetings of the noted Auftrian Committee at Paris during the fummer of 1792, till the tenth of Auguft
changed the face of things, were as regular and as well known
to the public as the meeting of the Cabinet-Council at St.
James's.

of

of the people; the circumftances of the times have enforced the neceffity of hardihood and frugality, and the abolition of that foe to great undertakings, luxury: the bravery, the fentiments of honour, the impatience of infult which formerly diftinguifhed them; are ftill cherifhed; while the charaƈteriftic levity, which counteraƈted the efficacy of thefe qualities, is converted by the fpirit of liberty into indefatigable perfeverance and unfhaken conftancy. Thefe effential alterations of charaƈter, though extraordinary, are not unaccountable: favorable opportunities and perilous contingencies have alternately confpired to mature the latent feeds of magnanimity; if profperity be the completion of the harveft, adverfity will have been the inftrument of cultivation.

The precipitation with which particular meafures have been carried, and the fanguinary cataftrophes, too frequently difgraceful to the caufe in which France is engaged, have excited deep regret in the bofoms of rational advocates for the rights of humanity, and vociferous reproaches from the mouths of penfioners on the corruptions of government. The exceffes, of which the champions for liberty have been guilty, have unblufhingly been adduced as justifications

juftifications of arbitrary encroachments: from
the misfortunes which have befallen an infant
republic, it has been argued that freedom is
dangerous under every form, and that the
eternal torments of inveterate defpotifm may
be better endured, than the temporary pur-
gatory of a revolution. But thefe outrageous
difputants fhould recollect, that candour invites
us to view the fair fide of every character; and
without engaging in the impious attempt of
vindicating cruelties, which from my foul I
abhor and lament, I muft affert that the general
conduct of the French during the prefent conteft has not affimilated itfelf to particular inftances of barbarity : but paying due refpect
to all reafonable objections againft them, I
fhall conclude my delineation of their prefent
features by pourtraying a remarkable trait:
that they feem determined to adhere to the
ftricteft forms of their new government in
the organization of their political and moral
fyftem ; that they are erecting the fuperftruc-
ture of their commonwealth on the venerable
foundations of Greece and Rome ; and that in
the republican aufterity of their principles
and practice, they approve themfelves the
emulous imitators of the examples afforded
by antiquity.

3   And

And are thefe pages to contain nothing but a bare-faced panegyric on our enemies? Would it not be the part of patriotifm rather to encourage the zeal of our countrymen by favorable reprefentations, than to damp their ardour in the purfuit of conqueft, by prognofticctions of fuccefs to their opponents? I cannot acquiefce in the juftice of fuch an objection. I know that it has been the policy of Minifterial partizans, to flatter the hopes of the country, by reprefenting the diftrefs and defpondency of the French as equal to their profligacy and enormities : to counteract the dangerous tendency of fuch bombaft, invented upon no fhadow of foundation, is worthy the endeavour of an advocate for peace : and I cannot help thinking, that a man, who reprefents the poffible and probable confequence of intemperate proceedings with a caution perhaps too earneft for the occafion, deferves better of the fociety to which he belongs, than another; who incites his fellow-citizens to exertions, the failure of which is deftruction, for the precarious attainment of vifionary benefits, originating and perhaps ending in the reveries of imagination. To acknowledge virtue, where it exifts in an adverfary, is the part of liberality : to fcrutinize the confequences of our own actions

with

with feverity, is the part of prudence and fortitude: no prejudice to our caufe can refult from the one; no difaffection to our country can be argued from the other. With thefe fentiments ever prefent to my mind, I fhall endeavour to draw practical conclufions from the recital I have made, and from other facts which I may be led to adduce: to fhew the benefit we may derive to our own intereft, from a juft apprehenfion of the enemy's character and circumftances; the only valuable end to which Effays of this kind can be directed.

And now, when the whole tenor of the Revolution is preffed on our recollection, what credit can we give to the affurances of thofe, who reprefent the French as on the point of capitulation? With what grace can we unite in fentiment with men, who laft year infpirited us with the fruitlefs hope of conquering, and this year confole us with the charitable project of ftarving, twenty-five millions of human beings? But are we to allow nothing for the refiftance, which thefe twenty-five millions of human beings will make againft the fubverfion of all, which they have been labouring to eftablifh? Are we to fuppofe that what has coft fo much time, fo much exertion, fo many lives,

will

will be relinquifhed in little time, with little
exertion, at the expence of but few lives?
Will the people of France confent, not to ga-
ther the fruits of what they have reared and
brought to maturity? Can it be imagined that
having firft overthrown the eftablifhed order of
things, they will affift in the re-eftablifhment
of that order? Poffeffions, which are labori-
oufly acquired, are wont to be anxioufly preferved; difficulty in attainment is feldom followed by facility in renunciation. Where
then is the profpect of termination to this
conteft? If we, with little apparent intereft
in the iffue, feel bold enough to proceed in fo
doubtful a career, will our adverfaries, who
are fighting *pro aris et focis*, not rival us in
perfeverance? Let us calculate the oppofition
we may expect from the refiftance we have
experienced. The moft prominent feature in
the Republican character as exhibited in France,
has been obferved to be prodigality of life.
Now this is a quality, which above all others
renders an individual formidable; when extended to a whole army or nation, it almoft
makes them invulnerable and irrefiftible. Indeed they virtually become fo; for as no inferior confiderations bias their actions, it is
only by extermination that victory can be
obtained,

obtained, when each individual prizes liberty above life. When only a few, when only thoufands cherifh this fentiment, it is poffible to deftroy the phalanx, and impofe the yoke of fubjeftion on an ignoble multitude: but when this fpirit becomes univerfal amongft millions; when not to feel it is infamy, when not to aft from it is treafon, the moft decided votaries of the confederate powers muft feel the impracticability of deftroying fuch a hydra.*

When we read the Conventional details of individual bravery, we feel animated and in-terefted : the heroifm of ancient times appears

---

* Mr. Mallet du Pan feems ftrongly impreffed with this fentiment, as the following, among many paffages in his " Confiderations," will fufficiently fhew.

" Ce ferait donc une méprife funefte de confidérer le dif-ferend aftuel, comme une guerre ordinaire de Puiffance á Puiffance, de compter excluſivement fur l'efficacité de la meil-lure armée, d'oppofer de vieilles régles á des conjonftures inovies, de combattre, par des mefures de routine, des hom-mes qui ont paffés tous les procédés connus, et de s'enfer-mer, pour y perir, dans un cercle de moyens dont une épre-uve, dangereufe á prolong'r, a déja manifefté l'infuffi-fance."

L   revived

revived among the moderns; the ideal ex-
ploits of the fabulous ages are verified in real
life. When we turn our attention to the
achievements of their armies, we feel more
forcibly the influence of fentiment on action:
at times we find them confounded by the fuperior difcipline of their adverfaries; we read
of thoufands flain in a fingle battle; of engagements which in common wars would have been
deemed decifive: but of what avail is this?
The routed forces rally; tens of thoufands
prefent themfelves to occupy the vacancy of
thoufands; the furvivors emulate the valour,
and court the fortune of the dead, and life is
only valued as it leads to victory. Thofe who
have examined the details of the two laft campaigns, even as given in our own Gazettes,
will be fenfible that this picture is not too
highly coloured: the conquefts which the
French have gained (to do juftice to the military character of the Combined Armies) have
not been eafy: their fuccefs has not been derived from the impetuofity of an onfet; they
have waded to victory through the blood of
their fellow-foldiers.

But a ftronger indication of the obftinacy
with which the ftruggle may be continued, is

2   the

the filent magnanimity with which they en-
counter difafters, and the tried fidelity with
which they have refifted temptation. To fuffer the miferies of life with patience, has been
accounted more heroic, than to die with fortitude: and this fpecies of heroifm has been
wonderfully exemplified by the French. Adverfity is more favorable to the human cha-
raēter than profperity: a remark juft in the
general, and particularly applicable to the
French. The unfhaken ftoicifm, with which
garrifons have at once witneffed the confla-
gration of their towns and the demolition of
their works; with which they have fuftained
the preffure of famine, is too well attefted to
need detail—the Britifh foldiery have borne
honorable teftimony to the defence of Valen-
ciennes; and the patriotic defperation of the
inhabitants of Landau, when exhaufted of the
ordinary means of fuftenance within, when
affailed by the inceffant operations of the
enemy from without, when enticed by the
flattering offer of falvation and recompence
on their furrender, will be honoured and ap-
proved by the univerfal fuffrage of unprejudiced pofterity. I have often been much
ftruck by the defcription of the French Pro-
teftants befieged in Rochelle by the French
King,

King, as given by Mrs. Macaulay in her Hiftory of England. The circumftances of this
fiege bear fo ftrong a refemblance to thofe attending the late fiege of Landau; the magnanimity exhibited on the two occafions is fo fimilar,
and the obfervation of the hiftorian fo well
deferving to be noticed, that I fhall tranfcribe
the paffage :

" Of twenty-two thoufand perfons who had
been fhut up in the town, four thoufand alone
furvived the hardfhips that they had undergone. The living not being in number fufficient, or in a condition to bury the dead,
vermin and birds of prey fed on the expofed
carcaffes. The dying carried their own coffins
into the church-yards, and there lay down and
breathed their laft. Rats, dogs, cats, mice,
human flefh, and other diftafteful food, had
been the only provifion on which thefe mar-
tyrs to the caufe of Religion and Liberty had
for fome time fed. The few inhabitants that furvived thefe miferies appeared like the fkeletons
of men. The ftory of their fufferings fhews
the mighty influence that virtue has over a
people actuated by a juft fenfe of Freedom,
that it not only over-balances every motive
of felf-prefervation, fubdues thofe frailties that
are

are infeparable from humanity, but raifes the mind abové the fenfe of evils that are the moft infupportable to the nature of man."

The attachment of the French foldiery to their country and Revolution, appears in a ftriking point of view on the defalcation of Dumourier. What were the expectations, what the difappointment of Europe on that occafion! When the news of that event arrived, it was immediately concluded, that from the General's popularity the troops would catch the contagion, remain attached to his Standard, and unite with him to crufh that liberty, they had fo nobly laboured to affert. Thofe conjectures were even magnified into certainty: and a rumor for fome time prevailed, that thefe converts to Ariftocracy were marching to Paris in a body. Dumourier indeed evidently reckoned on his influence over the minds of the Soldiers; and flattered himfelf that his talents of perfuafion could unfettle their attachment to the Republic. But as furrounding nations were aftonifhed, fo may they be inftructed by the behaviour of this patriotic army; with exceptions too inconfiderable to mention, they manifefted their zeal for the fervice of their country to be founded on
principle,

principle, and uninfluenced by the viciffitudes
of fortune. Though in circumftances of peril
the moft imminent, in which the military talents of their Commander could ill be fpared,
in which their own prefervation feemed to
depend on their adherence to him, they re-
fufed with generous indignation the treachery
propofed, and awaited the decifion of their
deftiny in the confcientious performance of
their duty. The difpaffionate fteadinefs difplayed on this occafion is rarely obfervable in
the conduct of large bodies : the feelings either
of approbation or difpleafure are ufually con-
tagious and violent ; the defertion of a leader
is calculated to excite a fpirit of revenge
among the objects of his treachery. But in
this inftance the fentiment of fidelity to their
obligations appeared admirably blended with
affection towards the partner of their labours ;
they continued at their pofts, but fuffered the
degraded chief to depart ; they refrained from
upbraiding his verfatility, but witneffed with
filent regret this unaccountable renunciation
of fame, fo anxioufly fought and fo defervedly
acquired.

The conduct of the National Convention,
whether on occafions of fuccefs or difappointment,

ment, cannot with propriety be overlooked: in the moment of victory, the folemnity with which they inftitute civic feftivals, the enthu- fiafm with which they congratulate the authors of their triumph, and the vivacity with which they participate in the rejoicings of the po- pulace, have a wonderful tendency to feed the flame of patriotifm among the citizens, and to infpire them with confidence at once in the pa- ternal care, and brotherly affection of their Reprefentatives. The addreffes which are from time to time circulated through the Departments and the Armies, are admirably adapted to diffeminate the Revolutionary principles, and infpire a meritorious intem- perance of courage amongft the Soldiers. The addrefs to the Army before Toulon* produced an almoft inftantaneous effect, in the alacrity with which the recapture of the place was ac- complifhed. The penman of that compofition

---

* This animated addrefs runs thus :

" Inhabitants of the Southern countries, you, into whofe fouls a fiery atmofphere has infufed generous paffions, and the burning enthufiafm that creates grand fuccefs," &c. &c.

For the compofition at full length, I refer my readers to the " Political State of Europe," vol. v. page 443.

exhibited

exhibited no inconfiderable knowledge of human nature; one of the ftrongeft paffions in the breaft of man is that of rivalfhip: this operates among individuals, but more ftrongly among nations; nor does it always originate in clafhing interefts or difcordant principles; it is often merely local, and exifts between the oppofite extremities of the fame community. The addrefs in queftion accommodates this local prejudice to the advantage of the public; after having enumerated and extolled the victories of the Northern Armies, in a ftrain of animation which muft warm every reader, it exhorts the men of the South not to be outdone by the inhabitants of a lefs favoured region: to fhew themfelves invigorated by the geniality of their climate, and as they carry off the prize from their brethren in the bounties of nature, to excel them in the ardor of enterprize. By fuch fuggeftions was popular enthufiafm wound to its higheft pitch; and the Britifh Minifter was precluded from boafting to Parliament of an event, which had been magnified by the hireling publications of the day as the moft brilliant of the campaign.

To pafs to the behaviour of the Convention under adverfe circumftances: though
philofophic

philofophic calmnefs among them is not fo furprifing, as in the promifcuous affemblage of an Army, it is equally beneficial in its effects. Defervedly as the exceffes, to which party animofity has given rife in that Affembly, have been reprobated, the tranquil dignity with which intelligence of difafters has been ufually fuftained, and the manly exertions by which the tranquillity of Paris has been preferved on fuch occafions, muft extort admiration from the moft prejudiced of their detractors. As an inftance in fupport of this remark, let the fituation of public affairs be confidered, at the time when the prefent Convention verified their Powers.

A fecond Revolution had juft taken place : the country had demanded a Republic, the Conftituted Authorities of the late Government were confequently fufpended, and time was requifite to fupply the deficiency with a legal fubftitution : perfonal fortitude and perfonal authority therefore in the new Delegates could only prevent the total diforganization of the fyftem. The change had been more critical and univerfal than that which took place in 1789. Then new modifications were introduced into the exifting Government : now both the

M   form

form and the fubſtance was deſtroyed, to be
created anew : the machinations of the adherents to Royalty were confequently to be ob-
viated, the concealed ambition of pretended
Champions for Republicanifm was to be fuppreffed, and the enormities of a defperate and
worthlefs band, who render periods of difficulty fubfervient to their own purpofes of
rapacity and violence, of whofe fury fuch me-
lancholy examples had recently been witneffed, were to be reſtrained.

Here one would think was fufficient employment for all good citizens; but to complete the accumulation of their diſtractions,
the enemy was advancing to their gates, and
the apprehenfions of civil difcord were abforbed in the imminence of that deſtruction,
by which a noble and populous city was to
expiate its offences, committed againſt Royalty.
But amidſt thefe multiplied calamities, the
fpirit of the Nation remained unbroken : the
Convention proceeded in the bufinefs allotted
them with united vigour and deliberation: they
employed themfelves in forming a Conſtitution, which the machinations of foreign
powers threatened to render abortive: they
gave its due fhare of attention to every meafure

fure which could infure internal tranquillity; they combated the fears and quickened the exertions of the multitude, and declared their refolution, that they would remain at their pofts, and be buried under the ruins of their Hall, fooner than defert the Metropolis, or betray the confidence of their Conftituents. Let not the prejudice of opinion, or reluctance to acknowledge the merits of an adverfary, withhold the approbation due to thefe inftances of patriotifm : let not the mention of facts, which are founded in reality, and will form a diftinguifhed chapter in the hiftory of mankind, be imputed to the finifter motive, of depreciating by comparifon the virtues of our countrymen ; but to a fincere defire of reprefenting exifting circumftances in their true colours, and carrying my fellow-citizens from the examination of truth to the knowledge of their true interefts.

Nor did the people at large neglect to emulate the conftancy of their Reprefentatives ; the cheerfulnefs with which all claffes, women as well as men, affifted to work in the entrenchments which were forming round Paris : the fortitude with which they fupported the idea of an enemy at the very barriers

of

of the Capital ; the obedience rendered to the decrees of the Convention, mark the determined character of this newly modelled people.

Nor can the scenes of tumult, which preceded or followed this epoch, invalidate the justice of the foregoing observations : the outrages to which I allude originated in different causes ; from the transactions of the 10th of August 1792, a suspicion had gone forth, that certain parties among the Citizens had conspired to deliver the country into the hands of the invaders ; hence arose the horrors of September. At enormities of this nature humanity shudders : but that the public indignation should be roused against the authors, real or supposed, of such a project, we cannot wonder, though our hearts recoil from the mode of executing vengeance : all men must regret, that the imputed criminality was not sifted and examined, and appropriate punishment inflicted on the offenders ; but that the innocent and the guilty were involved in one confusion, and fell victims to the temporary tyranny of anarchy. I must take occasion however to refute the calumnies by which the whole French Nation has been asperfed, in

consequence

confequence of thefe lamented tranfactions;
they have from hence been faid, as a people,
to be fanguinary and barbarous in their
difpofitions; but fuch a general conclufion
from the evidence of particular facts is a
libel, not upon the French, but upon human nature.* There is no nation under
the fun that deferves to be branded with
fuch an accufation; the force of intereft
or paffion may warp men from their
duty; the favage may be influenced to the
perpetration of murder by the dictates of
revenge, or for the poffeffion of a fkin;
the civilized barbarian may be induced, by
the temptations which corrupt governments
hold forth, to plot the deftruction of his
rival: but remove the temptation, remove

* So far is it from being true that the executions of September 1792, indicate the ferocious difpofition of Frenchmen
in general, that Englifh travellers who were in Paris at the
time declare, that the whole maffacre was perpetrated by not
more than fifty perfons. It will be confidered as difgraceful
to the public that fucl barbarities were not refifted; but
thofe who recollect the riots in London in 1780, will acknowledge that there is in all large bodies an aftonifhing
torpor, which prevents them from refifting the violence of
a defperate banditti; till compelled by the urgent neceffity
of felf-defence.

the

the fin that does moft eafily befet the individual or the nation, and you will not find
that God has dealt unequally by his crea-
tures, that he has granted a monopoly of
all the virtues to this or that nation, in
civilized or in savage life, or that he has
connected the true knowledge of himfelf
with an adherence to any particular fyftem
of human policy, as ftate-fanatics in their
unwife zeal have lately endeavoured to
evince.

To return to our particular cafe; either
fuch confpiracies were really formed, or the
charge was fabricated; if the plots exifted,
what wonder that the dregs of the people,
the refufe and fcorn of the community, by
whom thefe terrors were executed, fhould
be wrought on by their malicious and de-
figning leaders, to adopt danger as a pretext
for plunder? If fabricated, great was the
guilt of the fabricators; but the influence
of the fabrication on the minds of the populace, whom it deceived, was in proportion
to the confequences that would have attended the reality. The paffions of the people
have fince that time carried them to great
lengths on feveral occafions, and to a fe-

2   verity

verity of punishment unprecedented : this
effect is to be referred to civil diffenfions as.
its caufe; their profecution of the Emigrants,.
of the Rebels of La Vendée, of the Briffo-
tines, has been unrelenting ; for they have
confidered thefe factions as unnatural, becaufe domeftic enemies ; but it does not appear that they have treated prifoners of war,
with lefs humanity, than the oppofite party
have fhewn to theirs. But objections fuch
as thefe, allowing them to be juft, do not
affect my argument : I ftill aver that the
common caufe has been fupported with
energy ; that when the Duke of Brunfwick
was on his march to Paris, unanimity fprang
out of difcord : that the nation fhook off the
trammels of prejudice and party ; and that
every man at that moment laboured for the
one great object ; the fupport of national
independence and the extirpation of the invaders.

I have dwelt the longer on the civil
diffenfions of France, becaufe it is a ftrong
point in my argument, that we derive little
reafon for confolation or hope from thofe
diffenfions. When have the fquabbles of the
Convention paralyzed the activity of the
Armies ?

Armies? Even now, when the Sycophants
of the Minifter exult in the application of
the adage, " a houfe divided againft itfelf
cannot ftand," are not the French arms victorious in every quarter? Does not Germany
fhrink at their vicinity? A nation that can
fhew itfelf fo formidable amidft the contentions of party, will it not be ftill more
formidable if unanimity fhould enfue? If the
armies partake not the fpirit of diftruft and
infurrection, of what avail to us is the exiftence of that fpirit in remote provinces?*
But there is reafon to apprehend that we
are deceived in that particular: that parties
are confolidated in France, that the voice
of the Nation has confirmed the leaders of

* Cependant une année viént de s'écouler au milieu des
combats, et rien encore n'a fait flechir les refiftances! L'edifice eft lézardé par les fecouffes interieures, mais les colonnes
vacillantes ne perdent point leurs predeftaux. Pas une ville
n'ouvre volontairement fes portes ; pas un bataillon ne déferte
fes drapeaux, pas une armée ne céde le terrein fans le dif-
puter avec acharnement ; le cri de Royauté n'a pas encore
paffé la Loire inferieure ; le fanatifme s'alimente par les ca-
lamités ; les foldats meurent, d' autres les remplacent ; on
n'apperçoit ni terreur, ni laffitude, ni refipifcence. Mallet
du Pan, page 40.

the

the Mountain in their authority, and that the prefent fyftem is, with very few diffen-tients, the decided election of the people.

The circumftances which have lately been ad-duced in Parliament as reafons for the conti-nuance of the war, are fuch as, if juftly confi-dered, muft extinguifh the hope of crufhing the power of our Opponents. It has been argued, that the fupplies, which their Executive Go-vernment has hitherto obtained for carrying on their operations, muft foon fail ; the prin-ciple on which they are levied being unjuft in itfelf, and exciting revolt among the Ci-tizens. But where does this appear? The expedients which they have adopted feem likely to afford them refources for a long time to come ; and whatever an opulent Ariftocracy may think of their juftice, they cannot fail to accord with the fentiments of the multitude : fince the aim of the Legifla-ture has uniformly been, to proportion every man's burden to his ability ; to require from wealth contributions adequate to its fuper-fluities, that the narrow pittance of induf-trious poverty may not be invaded by the preffing neceffities of the times. An obfer-vation frequently made by Mr. Fox, " that

N

it

it is impoffible to devife productive taxes, that will not ultimately fall upon the lower claffes," is juft, as applied to our own, and other eftablifhed governments ; but means have been found in France to obviate this difficulty, which though generally reprobated as unjuft, I cannot find in my heart to cen- fure or regret: I mean heavy exactions from perfons known to be wealthy, and reftrictions on the indulgence of luxury. They have literally reduced to practice what Mr. Mar- tin, a refpectable Member, pleafantly fug- gefted to the Houfe of Commons : that rather than the poor man, who had only bread and cheefe, fhould be reduced to a cruft of bread alone, the National Reprefen- tatives, and other great men might be re- duced to dine on one courfe inftead of two.

To revert to the extraordinary refources of France : in the firft place, they have ap- propriated the gold and filver of the Churches to the expences of the community ; and for this act of facrilege they have been furi- oufly anathematized by the pious devotees of the Hierarchy, both in and out of Par- liament. But furely there was nothing fo
very

very exceptionable to the eye of reafon in this proceeding. What glory to God, what advantage to man could accrue from the fplendid baubles of fuperftitious ceremony? What fhould prevent the precious metals and ftones, which had been fequeftered for ages from all purpofes of utility, from being applied to the immediate exigencies of the ftate? But it is faid, the people had no right to feize on thefe valuables without the confent of their owners, the Clergy. A Legiflature appointed by the people are certainly juftified in arranging and diftributing property to the greateft benefit of the public: upon this principle it is that Acts of Parliaments are paffed for forming canals, or widening thoroughfares in cities: in which cafes the individual proprietors of lands or houfes are obliged to furrender their property to the community, to their private detriment, for an indemnification in their own opinion perhaps greatly infufficient. Upon this equitable principle a little extended, the appropriation of Ecclefiaftical ornaments might poffibly be juftified. But we may go upon different grounds; and with much propriety argue, that the Clergy had no property in them: they were of the

nature

nature of fixtures in the Church, placed there to expedite the reciprocal duties of the worſhipper and the officiating Miniſter. When the worſhippers wiſhed to transfer them, having no further uſe for them in their devotions, to civil purpoſes, what ground of complaint had the Prieſt, who was ſuppoſed to derive as little temporal benefit from ſilver ſaints and golden chalices as the Layman? It has turned out indeed, to the mortification of the prophane plunderers, that ſpiritual conſolation alone did not attach the Fathers to theſe objects of their adoration : many a bedizened Virgin of the Church has been ſtripped of her real Diamonds, and glittered in the almoſt equal ſplendor of Pariſian paſte. But whether the ſeizure of this property be conformable to juſtice or not, one thing is certain, in which we are materially concerned ; that the meaſure has enriched their Treaſury to a degree, which can hardly be credited but by thoſe, who have witneſſed the external magnificence, and are acquainted with the concealed ſtorehouſes of the Catholic Churches.

Another reſource ariſes from the rigor, with which perſons of real property are taxed for

for the maintenance of the Republic. This
has been alleged to be a future opening
for civil commotions, and but a tranfitory
advantage in the hands of the Convention.
Reafons have before been given for fuppofing, that the people will uphold their
Adminiftration in a meafure, which exone-
rates the induftrious from the partial feverity
of taxation: but the propofition from which
the foregoing inference is derived muft be
noticed ; no Minifter in this country would
dare to go fuch lengths againft the landed
and commercial interefts, which in fuch a
cafe would unite, and hurl him from his
feat of power: the ruling Powers in France
have deeply trenched upon the lawful rights
of thefe claffes, from a time-ferving predi-
lection towards the mob ; and thence it is
inferred that the time is at hand, when the
refpectable people of the country will join to
arreft the defperate courfe of a faction, and
reftore decency and fubordination in the
management of the National concerns. But
a contrary inference may with equal propriety be drawn from this circumftance : if
perfons, who from fuperiority of talents and
improvement, from the influence which property gives to every man among his neigh-
                                        bourhood,

bourhood, muſt neceſſarily acquire conſiderable weight in ſociety; if ſuch perſons have not oppoſed theſe requiſitions of the Executive Power with all their influence, if they have been contented to endure more than perſons of their own ſtation in other countries would endure; what I would aſk is the cauſe of theſe conceſſions, but that this phantom of liberty is to their deranged optics a ſubſtance; that they do not feel themſelves grievouſly afflicted, by what we conſider as the miſeries of their ſituation? Much has been ſaid about the means employed to keep the country in ſubjection: but that the nation, which can ſhew itſelf ſo powerful againſt foreign invaders, ſhould be unable to cruſh its domeſtic oppreſſors, if it ſaw them in the light of oppreſſors, is an inconſiſtency for which I cannot account.

The ſame deference to the Convention, which appears on the ſubject of finance, may be obſerved in other branches of the Government, in all the proceedings of the Citizens. In obedience to the decrees of the Legiſlature, Generals have been arreſted at the head of their Armies, and carried before the tribunal of juſtice: no murmur has been
heard

heard againſt the authority which directed the meaſure; no mutiny has enſued from the attachment of the Soldiers to their caſhiered Officers, or from the hardſhips of the ſervice to themſelves: no inſtance can be adduced in which a Regiment has refuſed to face the enemy, or to ſupply with the enthuſiaſm of courage the deficiency of numbers or of diſcipline. In vain does the Britiſh Miniſter aſſert, that theſe exertions, which he confeſſes to be extraordinary, muſt be of ſhort duration, as proceeding ſolely from the fear of the Guillotine. Whence does this fear of the Guillotine ariſe? Who has the directions of its operations? The people of whom the armies are a part. Their bravery Mr. Pitt avers to be the effect of terror. What ſhould terrify an armed nation? What are Danton* and Roberſpierre, what the Convention, unleſs ſupported by the People? They have no force, no authority but the approbation of their Conſtituents: why then do not thoſe Conſtituents, marſhalled in military array, nſtead of combating, aſſiſt the friendly intentions of the

* This queſtion has recently been anſwered by the Revolutionary Tribunal.

3   Combined

Combined Powers, ſubvert the inſtitutions of their unprotected Legiſlators, and reſtore the ancient eſtabliſhment, for which in their hearts they languiſh? The fact is, they do not languiſh for the reſtoration of Deſpotiſm: they do not feel towards the Convention as we think they feel; they approve the changes that have taken place, and will uphold the new ſyſtem to the utmoſt of their abilities.*

But the moſt ſtriking proof of the Conventional Power, is the decree of requiſition. This was a bold and unprecedented meaſure: and as ſuch was the ſubject of cavil and ridicule all over Europe, and its execution conſidered to involve an impoſſibility. But impoſſibilities have more than once been realized by the French; and the

---

* To ſhew the ſmall hopes which ſenſible writers on the ſide of the Royaliſts entertain from a Counter Revolution, M. Mallet du Pan makes the following obſervation on the term " contre-revolution; mot qui impliquant le retabliſſement abſolu de tout ce qui a eté changé ou aboli, devait être proſcrit au moins par la prudence, et qui, devenu le ſignal du fanatiſme, a donné plus de bras a la République que la cocarde tricolore." Conſiderations, page 50.

effects

effects with which this meafure has been attended, are at once unexpected and alarming.
It was foretold, that thefe newly-raifed multitudes, undifciplined and refractory, would
only create confufion in the ranks, and expedite the ruin of the caufe; but thefe objects of fcorn and laughter have defeated
the moft experienced Generals, and put to
flight the beft appointed Armies of the
prefent times : nor is there any occurrence
during the progrefs of this hard-fought conteft, that has fo entirely thwarted the meafures of the Combination, as the infurrection
of the People en maffe.* The late alarming fucceffes which they have obtained, have
extorted from a plaufible Orator in Office
the unfortunate confeffion, that they are an
armed nation ; which is tantamount to a
confeffion that they are invincible.

Much has lately been faid refpecting a

* Lorfque la Convention rendit ce décret digne de Xercés,
par lequel elle ordonnait une levée fubite et extraordinaire de
300,000 hommes, on riàit de mepois, et la raifon le jufti-
fiait. Cependant, cette armeé fublidiaire s'eft formée en
trés grande partie, au milieu de murmures fans effet, et de
méc ontentemens fans energie. Mallet du Pan, page 43.

O   deficiency

deficiency of arms and ammunition, and
concerning a fcarcity of provifions; the affertion refpecting arms is untrue, as 300,000
ftand of arms have been delivered to the
People in the fpace of one year; with regard to the articles of ammunition and provifions, the truth of report cannot eafily be
afcertained; but with regard to the former,
the late arrival of fhips from India has probably, thanks to the indefatigable diligence
of the Britifh Admiralty, furnifhed them with
the neceffary fupply of falt-petre: and the
vigorous meafures which the Committee of
Public Safety are taking for the prevention
of luxurious wafte, for a regular fupply,
and an equal diftribution of provifions, feem
likely to remedy thofe temporary difficulties,
which monopoly rather than fcarcity muft
have occafioned; fince the fruits of a plentiful harveft laft year, and the general cultivation of corn or potatoes in grounds which
were formerly laid out as Gardens or Parks,
muft have tolerably fupplied the deficiency
of importation.

Much ridicule has been employed in defcribing the bare condition of the Sans-Culotte
armies: but perfons, who by having vifited
the

the fcene of action may be allowed to form a fair judgment, have afferted that the French are better provided in the article of clothing than any troops in the field ; not-withftanding the Ladies of Great-Britain have lately figured in the capacity of Army-Tailors.

To fum up the catalogue of their advantages, their fuperiority in the knowledge of engineering is acknowledged throughout Europe; their attainments in philofophy and ufeful arts are known to be unrivalled; and what is moft extraordinary, the labours of their celebrated Academy have been profe-cuted with unabated diligence, throughout the progrefs of this inveterate conteft. In fhort, when we confider that we are en-countering opponents, whofe refources are fo numerous as to be incalculable ; all whofe refinements of art and difcoveries of fcience are converted into inftruments, for augmenting the terrors of their prowefs, we muft confefs the hazard to be fearful, and the advantages of fuccefs inadequate to be balanced againft the probable confequences of defeat. Thofe fplendid exertions, which the Government of this Country has treated

as

as cafual and tranfitory, are now by continuance and repetition refolved into fyftem;
thofe hopes, which the capture of one or
two frontier towns excited in the early part
of the campaign, have been defeated by the
repulfes which the Combined Armies have
recently experienced on the borders of the
Rhine: notwithftanding the victories pro-
claimed in Minifterial harangues, not a fingle doubt can be entertained by unprejudiced perfons, but that the condition of the
whole Confederacy has fuffered confiderable
deterioration fince the commencement of the
war. Much as we exult in the events of
the Campaign, the French exult equally in
thofe events: their fpirits, in fpite of the
famine which is faid to ftare them in the
face, are buoyed up with the moft animating fentiments; their alacrity appears redou-
bled in the profecution of their object; their
madnefs, if fuch it be, has method in it:
they feem to have refolved on the extinction
of perfonal pique and interefted animofity;
on the reftoration of that unanimity, by
which the firft Revolution was rendered fuccefsful, and on a final pacification on no
other terms, than the recognition of their fovereignty as a nation.

CHAP.

CHAP. III.

RECAPITULATION.

THUS have I traced the circumſtances in which this country and France ſtand, as oppoſed to each other in a ſtate of warfare: and it is neceſſary here to obſerve, that any invidious parallel between the Conſtitutions of the two countries, in regard to their nature or influence over the public mind, has been carefully avoided: ſuch points only have been touched upon, as loudly call for inveſtigation from every friend to his country; the diſcuſſion of which can afford no reaſonable cauſe for offence, to the moſt zealous aſſerter of limited monarchy. Before I draw towards a concluſion, it will be proper for the ſake of perſpicuity to bring my comparative ſtatement of circumſtances to one point. On the one hand, we have ſeen all the leading powers of Europe riſing in arms againſt a ſingle nation: on the other, that ſingle nation, fired with enthuſiaſm, preparing to reſiſt ſo formidable a combination.

tion. As action fucceeded to preparation, we have feen the progrefs of the united powers impeded by contrariety in the obje&t of their different purfuits; by thofe fermentations which always take place, when a temporary alliance is formed between interefts naturally difcordant for the attainment of a prefent obje&t: we have feen the French retaliating invafion on the invaders, fimply by the force of unanimity and confidence: we have heard of Auftrians and Pruffians more inimical to each other than to the French, and we know that we are bound by treaty to indemnify our Allies for the defence of their own territories: we find our enemies on the contrary burying the meaner feelings of perfonal confideration in the difinterefted fervice of their country; neither fubfidizing nor fubfidized, but depending for their prefervation on the patriotifm of their fellow-citizens: difcipline on the one hand has yielded to impetuofity, impetuofity on the other has learnt from experience the leffon of difcipline: the motives of a&tion being indefinite in one party, the meafures that have been adopted have been complicated in their plan, and unfuccefsful in their execution: independence and fecurity being

being the definite motives of the other party, they have been enabled to proportion their means to their end ; all their operations have been on a fimple, and though extenfive, practicable fcale ; the effect correfponding to the defign, and fatally convincing the incredulity of their antagonifts.

When we contraft the civil condition of the two countries, we experience a remarkable diffimilarity : on the one hand burdens are increafed, while refources are diminifhed; while trade and manufactures languifh and decline, the connections of great and noble families are enriched by the fpoils of war, and penfions to the third and fourth generation annexed to offices, of which the duties were deftined to laft but for three or four months : on the other, the preffure of neceffary expences alleviated, by abolifhing the luxurious profufion of a Court, and fuppreffing the redundant privileges of a Priefthood and Nobility ; the moft exalted fervices rewarded with civic honours, and the peculation of office facrificed to the enjoyment of public confidence and applaufe. On the one hand, a luxurious nation, as England is become throughout all but the

lowelt

loweſt claſſes of ſociety; where the conve-
niences and elegancies of life are more generally cultivated and more highly prized
by the middling ranks than in any country
in Europe; where the progreſs of luxury
ſeems too likely to undermine the manli-
neſs of the national character; on the other
hand, a country, where not only luxury, but
comfort was formerly monopolized by the
Ariſtocracy of the land; where the maſs of
the people, inured to miſery without proſpect of melioration or relief, can the more
patiently undergo the hardſhips to which they
have been accuſtomed, and refrain from the gra-
tifications not yet matured for their enjoyment,
when they reflect that the harveſt, in which
they have hitherto only laboured, is about to
yield its produce to themſelves; when they
conſider that they have every thing to gain,
and their Antagoniſts every thing to loſe.

This compariſon is unfavorable to the pre-
valent opinions and wiſhes of the time; but
for its juſtice the only appeal that can be
made, is to the feelings and ſober reflection
of the public at large; and to thoſe who
view the ſubject in that light in which it is
here repreſented, it may with propriety be
urged,

urged, that their duty towards their fellow-citizens requires them to put forth every ex-ertion, confiftent with the regulations of fo-ciety and their condition in life, to bring to a fpeedy termination, a conteft, in which the moft important interefts of Great-Britain and of mankind are fo prodigally facrificed to the vifionary projects of Statefmen.

P   C H A P.

CHAP. IV.

CONCLUSION.

RELYING with fome degree of confidence on the validity of the foregoing affertions, I will endeavour from the retrofpection of the paft, to chalk out the path of prudence for the future.

What is the object to which men of all defcriptions and opinions, however zealous for
the profecution of the war, however unreafonable in their expectations of fuccefs, direct
their ultimate attention? Peace. None are fo
fenfelefs or fo frantic, as to deny that war is
a calamity: we cannot but fuppofe that it is
univerfally confidered as an evil, in which
nothing fhort of indifpenfible neceffity fhould
involve a nation; the fpeedy conclufion of
which, when once incurred, fhould occupy
the united endeavours of all parties, and conftitute the prime wifh of every refpectable
character in public or in private life. What
then are the means by which peace may be
obtained? The following is the alternative;
abfolute

abſolute conqueſt, or reciprocal negotiation :
with regard to the former, if there be any
truth in the preceding remarks, the total im-
probability of ſuch an iſſue muſt be acknowledged.

And are we to be reduced to deſpair by difficulties and objeſtions, conjured up in the
chimerical imagination of an unknown pam-
phleteer ? The ſeeming impoſſibility attending
the conqueſt of France does not reſt on ſo
ſandy a foundation ; the rationality of the aſ-
ſertion, that a country, ſo ſtrongly fortified by
nature and by art ; ſo formidable by its po-
pulation, and ſo fertile in its interior reſources,
will be capable of repelling the moſt powerful
invaders from its territory, has been atteſted
by military men of the moſt conſummate ſkill,
and the ſtrongeſt predileſtion for the land of
their nativity. The opinions of thoſe ſturdy .
Politicians, who plan the victorious operations
of an offenſive war in the Box of a Coffee-
Houſe, are in this inſtance refuted by the
authoritative teſtimony of a Duke of Marl-
borough ; by the juſt and concluſive reaſon-
ings of a General Lloyd, and by the perſonal
experience of a Duke of Brunſwick : a ſtream
of authorities, which our warlike Adminiſtration

tion have hitherto attempted to oppofe: but
now, when not the labours of a whole Campaign, nor even the Generalfhip of the firft
Law Lord in the Kingdom, have been able to
produce any material impreffion on that impracticable Frontier, even they begin to perceive the errors of their fyftem, and to de-
fpair of its fuccefs: and unlefs the calamities
of famine fhould opportunely interpofe for
their affiftance, they will be confiderably em-
barraffed to procure fuftenance for the hopes
of their partizans, who daily feed on the Continental miferies, fo minutely defcribed in the
authentic correfpondence of the Treafury
Newfpapers.

Since then the movers and conductors of
hoftilities, together with the moft experienced
profeffors of military fcience, are unable any
longer to indulge the expectation of conqueft,
the road to peace can lead only through negotiation : a meafure, which, had it been adopted in the commencement of the rupture, might
have prevented all thofe embarraffments, commercial and civil, which have been fo preju-
dicial to the mercantile interefts of the Kingdom, and fo diftreffing to the feelings of
national patriotifm. But it is in vain to dwell

3

on

on the miftakes of the paft; their mention is impertinent, except as it leads to the correction of the future: but the inconveniences we have already fuffered from the omiffion of a duty fhould ftimulate us to the performance of it with the greateft alacrity. That a negotiation muft finally take place between ourfelves, and the nation with whom we are embroiled, we are fully fatisfied: how great foever may be our pride, however lofty our ambition, in the prefent complicated ftate of our Finances, "to this compleftion we muft come at laft."

That we muft ultimately negotiate has been acknowledged by the Minifter: but will any man fay that the prefent is the proper feafon for negotiation? Whatever may be the fentiments of the ftatefman on the fubjeft, the Moralift will argue, that the immediate is the moft fuitable time for accomplifhing a juft and laudable purpofe: and there is every reafon to believe, that morality will not on this, or on any other occafion, be found to be at variance with policy. We might, if the fetters of alliance and the inflexibility of punftilio impeded not the exercife of our underflandings, accommodate our unfortunate differences with

as

as much convenience and advantage to ourfelves at the prefent, as at any future period:
that we fhould come off victorious in a conteft,
to which our powers are utterly unequal, in
which we feem to be contending againft the
appointments of Providence and the conftitution of humanity, is a fuppofition too romantic
to be indulged; and if this be not the cafe, there
appears no probability, that our circumftances
will hereafter be more favourable than at prefent
to a happy termination: but on the contrary,
fhould the progrefs of the French arms remain
uninterrupted, fhould the current of fortune
continue to flow with their bark, it is more than
poffible, we may hereafter be compelled to
meafures, which now we might voluntarily,
and therefore creditably adopt: the cataftrophe
of the American tragedy may be repeated, and
the retraction of our lordly manifeftoes be
ftipulated, as a preliminary to the defired
accommodation.

Nor will it be confidered by the friends of
humanity as a trivial argument, in favour of a
fpeedy pacification, that by this method only
can that effufion of blood be prevented, by
which the territories of the aggreffors and the
aggrieved are equally depopulated, and the
members

members of the ſtate, its moſt valuable trea-
ſure, diſperſed and deſtroyed with unfeeling
prodigality.

But do not obſtacles exiſt, which render a
preſent treaty dangerous if not impracticable?
I can diſcover no obſtacles which a willing diſpoſition may not eaſily ſurmount. It has been
aſſerted with much confidence, that our ſolemn
declarations, made on the faith of the nation
to our allies, and the preſervation of order ſo
neceſſary to the welfare of ſociety, conſpire to
form an inſurmountable objection againſt the
eſtabliſhment of peace, while the government
of France remains in the hands of the preſent
leading men : men who, neither reverencing
the Omnipotence of Heaven, nor reſpecting
the ordinances of civil ſociety, aſſume the habit
of Liberty as a covering to their ambition, and
having involved the land of their nativity in
irremediable calamity, are panting to deſtroy
throughout the world the wiſe inſtitutions of
their forefathers, and to eſtabliſh on the foundation of unbridled licentiouſneſs the ſecond
reign of anarchy and barbariſm. If our Governors have really pledged us to a meaſure
of ſo doubtful an iſſue, as that of waging war
to the extermination of certain parties or principles,

ciples, entertained and fupported in a foreign
country, unprecedented has been their te-
merity : if our comrades require the performance of our engagements in their fulleft
extent, we may be held to perfevere in this
fatal enmity from year to year, till domeftic
calamity, confpiring with foreign machinations,
may reduce us to the brink of ruin, and our
pertinacity engage us to the commiffion of political fuicide. But let us hope we are not fo
deeply involved, and that the prefervation of
our civil exiftence will never be found incompatible with the line of conduct to which we
are bound : fhould that ever be our unhappy
cafe, miferable will be their lot, who witnefs
the commotions and conflicts of thofe times.

Not fuppofing that we are further engaged
than prudence warrants, or that thofe, to whom
the Conftitution has intrufted the Difcretionary
Power of war or peace, have been fo impru-
dent as to diveft themfelves of that power, I
will proceed to notice the argument againft
prefent negotiation, which refts upon the characters and views of the political leaders in
France. Whether they really meditate fuch
diabolical defigns as are imputed to them, of
erecting a bloody anarchy on the ruins of
                                        focial

focial fubordination, may with fome fhew of
reafon be doubted; that their countrymen do
not fufpect them of fuch intentions, is fufficiently evident from the cordiality with which
they are fupported by a numerous majority:
for that the body of inhabitants in any diftrict
or realm fhould coincide in fo prepofterous a
fyftem, or imagine that they could have an
intereft in fubverting the ufeful regulations of
a community, and poifoning the bleffings of
'civilization with the infufion of fyftematic
violence and barbarity, is a fuppofition too
wild and chimerical to be countenanced by
any philofophic reafoner. Such unnatural
fchemes may be engendered in the brain of
an afpiring demagogue: but the monfters will
ever be deftroyed in the moment of their birth,
by the juft abhorrence of an enlightened
·people, impelled by the dictates of reafon and
.nature; and in the eftablifhment of their own,
providing for the maintenance of univerfal
Liberty.

But granting the epithets beftowed upon
French Legiflators to be merited, I deny that
from the unworthinefs of their characters a
conclufion may be fairly drawn, that it would
be unadvifable in our prefent circumftances to

Q   treat

treat with them. Mr. Burke has endeavoured to irritate the minds of the Englifh againft the French, and extinguifh their defire for mutual amity and good will, by brandifhing a theatrical dagger in the Houfe of Commons; in his writings and fpeeches he has arranged his machinery with confiderable art, and produced his Pantomimical horrors with effect; but however fuccefsfully he may have exerted his power over the human feelings, a power which notwithftanding his eccentricities he eminently poffeffes, it ftill remains true, that with the perpetrators of thefe enormities we muft at laft enter into an accommodation.

But let us enter a little into the confequences which would refult from the general admiffion of the principle laid down on this particular occafion. When we are convinced that the termination of a war will be expedient for our own interefts, are we to prolong its calamities to ourfelves, till the reformation and repentance of our enemy fhall have rendered him worthy to participate in the bleffings of peace? Are we become fuch formidable champions in the caufe of morality, that we fhould exhauft our own ftrength, and endanger our own fecurity, rather than fuffer the wickednefs of our

neighbour

neighbour to remain unpunifhed? No peace
can be effected with honour or with fafety, till
the prefent ambitious and unprincipled Adminiftration of France is difplaced. If this
maxim is to be erected into a general rule, if
no treaty of peace or commerce is to be concluded between two nations, without an un-
deniable certificate can be obtained that the
parties are actuated by honourable and equitable motives, the horrors of war may be
perpetuated from generation to generation,
and the inhabitants of each feparate region be
unfociably infulated within the limits of their
refpective territories. If, before we negotiate
with the Minifters of a foreign country, we are
to require the feverity of moral rectitude, and
the perfection of political integrity and candor
at their hands, can we reafonably expect ever
to negotiate? Are thefe valuable qualities
liberally implanted in the breafts of States-
men? Are we certain that the fucceeding routine of Governors in France will foar nearer to
the fummit of our expectations than the prefent?
Have we been equally fcrupulous in afcertain-
ing the difinterefted philanthropy of our Allies, as in probing the moral turpitude of our
Antagonifts? Have the members of the Cabinet at St. James's afforded a fplendid example
of

of Minifterial incorruptibility, and thus eftablifhed their right to affume the offices of cen-
fors, to pafs judgment on the character and
conduct of the Diplomatic world? Woe be
to you, ye foreign Ambaffadors, Emigrants, or
Military fchemers, who crowd the Office of
the Minifter to confult on the affairs of war,
if ye approach that holy place with unclean
hands or polluted hearts; thefe Puritans of
State, thefe auftere Round-heads of the political world have declared in the face of the
whole nation, that " they would rather choofe
to perfevere in the war even amidft the worft
difafters, and fhould deem fuch a conduct
much more fafe and honourable, than to conclude a peace with the ruling powers in France
upon their prefent fyftem :"* doubtlefs becaufe
it is a fyftem of immorality and injuftice. Beware then how you yield to the temptations
of ambition, left you incur the virtuous difpleafure of the Britifh Adminiftration : divide
the fpoil of Poland among ye quietly, it fhall
be overlooked ; drive the harmlefs, but befot-
ted Turk from his feat of Empire, the violence fhall be pardoned : thefe are venial of-

* Vide Mr. Pitt's Speech on the opening the prefent
Seffion.

fences :

fences: but afpire to put the multitude in poffeffion of their rights, attempt to aggrandize
your King and Country, by fecuring the liberty and property of your fellow-citizens
from the ftrides of power, or connive at fuch
dangerous ambition in others, and you fhall
be denounced as innovators on the fettled forms
of governments, as enemies to the eftablifhed
fubordination of fociety, as Demagogues and
Enthufiafts, Atheifts and Affaffins.

But if we defcend from the fublimities, into
which the nice feelings of thefe Moralifts
elevate them, and examine the plain truth,
we fhall be convinced that this ideal ftandard
of integrity is never fet up, but when fome
private purpofes are to be ferved. The prefent
rulers of France are unworthy to negotiate
with the Britifh Minifter, becaufe the Britifh
Minifter does not think it to his prefent purpofe to negotiate with them ; but fhould he
in the courfe of time alter his opinion, and
wifh to prevent " the worft difafters" by con-
cluding a peace, he would then difcover it to
be fufficient, that any fet of men are at the head
of affairs in a country with which we are embroiled, however they may have attained that
fituation, or however they may conduct them-

felves in it, to warrant us in adopting such arrangements with them, as may appear to be for the interefts of our own community. There is a palpable abfurdity in the affectation of difdaining to treat with any potentate, who is in a condition to levy war againft us : it is not the honour or punctilio of this party or that, which is to be confulted, but the permanent benefit and happinefs of the nations which are engaged in the conteft. Are we then to negotiate with ruffians ? with banditti ? Yes. Let us remember to hold their vices in abhorrence, and we fhall not be contaminated by their intercourfe.

But the moft material objections to negotiation remain to be anfwered ; the declaration on the part of France of eternal war againft Monarchy, and the refolution againft treating with any power, which occupies the fmalleft part of their territory, or refufes to acknowledge the independent fovereignty of their Republic. With refpect to the firft article of this charge, the decree which declared war againft all the eftablifhments of Europe was either the offspring of infanity or of artifice : it originated either in the romantic fcheme of confolidating all Europe into one immenfe Republic,

public, a fcheme which from its notorious impracticability required not a ferious oppofition, or, as has been ftrongly fufpected, in
the criminal defign of affording a fpecious plea
to the furrounding powers, who were waiting
for an opportunity to join the Germanic combination. Be it what it might, it perifhed in
the grave of its Authors. The predominant
party of the prefent day did at the time, and
do ftill exprefs their hearty difapprobation of
that obnoxious meafure of univerfal fraterni-
zation, and went fo far as to adopt it as a
leading accufation againft that ill-fated faction.
It is well known to all who acquaint themfelves with the affairs of France, that the Convention have exprefsly declared their determination, not to interfere with the internal
arrangements of other countries, but to affert
their own inviolability, and proceed againft
their enemies, not by argument and perfuafion, but by terror and violence.

I cannot conceive what grounds a repealed
decree can afford for declining to negotiate ;
but ftill the ambition of the Convention and
their appetite for conqueft is reiterated, and it
is afferted from high authority that any peace
that we could obtain in the prefent circumftances,

ftances, would be but a tranfitory and delufive calm.

In our negotiations with Monarchical States we have never found, nor did we ever expect to find, that the pacific engagements, into which we have been induced to enter, would be regarded inviolable, like the laws of the Medes and Perfians : but this circumftance of poffible inftability has never operated as an objection againft fuch engagements, when the policy of the government has favoured their formation. Why then fhould we be fo deli-cately fcrupulous in our meafures towards a Republic, unlefs it be true, that there is an implacable animofity againft Republicanifm in the attendants and Minifters of Monarchy?

But it is idle to avoid a defirable and ne-ceffary peace, from the apprehenfion that the ambition of our Antagonifts may induce them to infringe its articles at a future period. Surely we may place equal dependence on the faith of the Convention, as on the faith of Louis the XIVth, or any other Monarch of France ; princes, who have been generally actuated in their conduct by a thirft of univerfal dominion, and a reftlefs jealoufy of Britifh greatnefs. It
has

has been faid by the Official Orator of the Houfe of Commons, that the afpiring views of Louis the XIVth, were accompanied with exalted fentiments of honour, that noble and humanizing principle which predominates in the actions of Kings, and reconciles the paffion for abfolute fway with the interefts of civilization: but the views of aggrandizement entertained by the modern Republicans are founded in felfifhnefs and fenfuality, thofe unworthy feelings of ignoble minds, which influence them to reduce the fuperiority of refined fociety to their own plebeian level, to deftroy the beautiful creations of art throughout the cultivated world, and wreft the difcoveries of fcience to the eftablifhment of popular tyranny and political fanaticifm. This contraft between Monarchical and Republican ambition may ferve to difcover to the public the principles of its author, but will produce no conviction in the minds of confiderate and unprejudiced perfons.

Precedent being the rule by which it is the cuftom of modern times to regulate actions, let us confider whether it has been ufual for the Conductors of public counfels to proceed upon thefe arbitrary and fophiftical diftinctions.

R   There

There is no period in the Annals of Great-Britain, in which the alliance of England has been more univerfally courted,* than during the continuance of the Commonwealth : nor did the Minifters of the furrounding Potentates, though for the moft part devoted to the caufe of defpotifm, imagine that the fyftem, which prevailed among the leading party here, afforded them any reafonable grounds for kicking againft the pricks, and hazarding a conteft with fo formidable a rival.

Granting all this to be true, and that we have equal reafon to expect the obfervance of engagements from the prefent Government of France, as from an arbitrary power, they ftill argue the inexpediency of prefent Negotiation from the haughty behaviour affumed by the Republic. Let any overture be made on the

---

* "Never did the annals of humanity furnifh the example of a government, fo newly eftablifhed, fo formidable to foreign ftates as was at this period the Englifh commonwealth. To Republics the object of envy, to Monarchs of hate, to both of fear, it was affiduoufly courted by all the powers of Europe. London was full of Ambaffadors, to endeavour, for their refpective fuperiors, to excufe former demerits, to renew former treaties, and to court ftricter alliances with England." Macaulay's Hiftory of England. vol. v. chap. iii.

part

part of England or her Allies; the French, encouraged by their late fucceffes, and relying on the energy of their new character, might not improbably be induced to reject all conciliatory propofals, or accept them only on terms fo humiliating to their Adverfaries, as to give a fevere wound to the delicacy of Britifh honour, and degrade us from the exaltation to which we have defervedly been raifed in the fcale of European nations. Thefe are the unfounded arguments of pride; of that haughtinefs in ourfelves which we condemn in others: let the conditions we propofe be fuch, as may be honourable for us to offer, and creditable for them to accept, and there is no reafon to believe that they are fo enamoured of the calamities infeparable from war, as to fi urn our liberal advances; or if they do, fo far fhall we be from fuffering a diminution of our dignity by an unmerited repulfe, that we fhall have made known to the world the moderation of our views, fhall have refcued our conduct from the imputation of mercenary motives, and have given a colour of juftice to our attempting by force thofe objects, which we have previoufly failed to attain by perfuafion.

3   But

But let my meaning be fully underftood when I recommend a propofal of accommodation : their advantage muft be confulted equally with our own fchemes of policy ; we muft be equally tender of their independence, as tenacious of our own importance ; the reciprocal privileges of nations, the general good of fociety, the imprefcriptible rights of humanity muft form the bafis of reconciliation ; the narrow views of partial aggrandizement muft be abforbed in the purfuit of univerfal happinefs, and the determinations of Cabinets and Courts for once muft derive their tone from the principles of juftice and philofophy. If we cannot prevail on ourfelves to proceed on this fcale of magnamity, if we cannot facrifice fomething of local and political prejudice to the promotion of philanthropy and peace ; to adopt the foregoing advice upon a contracted plan, to negotiate upon Machiavelian ideas with a Republic, will indeed be a fruitlefs attempt, and fubject our unacceptable propofals to the infult of rejection.

Suppofe it to be true that views of conqueft are concealed under the mafk of liberty and independence, I do not fee why thofe views may not be more conveniently fruftrated by negotiation.

negotiation, than by arms; in a state of tranquillity we shall find leisure to fortify ourselves against their attacks, and to counteract the effects of their secret machinations; by protracting the period of hostilities, we incur the danger of debilitating our strength; we are led to adopt the pernicious policy of replacing our compatriot defenders, sent to be initiated in the discipline of despots, by the introduction of foreign mercenaries; we make the future prosperity of our country, nay, perhaps, the very existence of our valued Constitution, to depend on the event of a battle or the vicissitudes of a campaign.

But the opening of a treaty is to be preceded by the vacation of the enemy's territory; a circumstance which renders the very idea of pacification romantic and absurd.—Whatever it may be policy in us to determine upon this subject, to demand this concession, in them was wisdom; to treat with an enemy in possession of their frontier, would be to submit to the will of a master; to sign their own sentence of dismemberment. But shall we relinquish all the advantages we have gained, and then condescend to a negotiation? If the advantages

we

we have gained will purchafe us a fafe and honourable peace, and liberate us from the perplexity in which we are involved, we fhall part with them for more than their value. For what are thefe advantages? We have been nibbling at the Northern boundaries of France for a twelvemonth, and have pilfered a town or two, which have been delivered to the Emperor: we have fhared the labours of the campaign, and transferred the fcanty profits to our Allies; we have equipped a tremendous fleet, and expofed our trade unprotected to our enemies.

But we have greater objects in our view, than the poffeffion of a few Garrifon towns on the Continent; we wifh to preferve the acqui-fition of territory which we have already attained in the Eaft-Indies, and hope to in-demnify ourfelves for the expences we have incurred by the capture of the French Iflands in the Weft. I am not furprifed that fuch fhould be the policy of Minifters; this fpecies of indemnification muft ever be confonant with their purpofes; acceffion of patronage confti-tutes the milk and honey of thefe promifed lands: but that the independent part of the community

community fhould be influenced by fuch motives, and co-operate with the dividers of the fpoil in the fupport of a deftructive war, for the profecution of defigns, the utmoft fuccefs of which will create no advantage to the people at large, will caufe no augmentation of our natural refources, nor add a fingle article to the domeftic comforts of the poor, appears unaccountable upon any known principles of common fenfe. The idea that national profperity is advanced by foreign conquefts, has long been exploded from the creed of reafon ; free commerce with diftant countries is acknowledged to be more beneficial in its effects than the exercife of fovereignty ; and thofe commodities both of ufe and luxury, which we derive from our Trans-Atlantic Empire, would come to us upon much eafier terms, if every ifland were declared independent. Why then fhould we lay fuch ftrefs on the retention of conquefts, the glory of which is dubious, and the benefit nominal? Our advantages being fo inconfiderable, the difgrace of relinquifhing thofe advantages muft be proportionably fmall ; though there are who think that by a voluntary refignation of our pretenfions, while yet there is any merit in the conceffion, we fhall moft effectually confult our own intereft and reputation,

tation, and thus obviate that compulfory termination of our efforts, to which the moft formidable nation or confederacy of nations is eventually deftined, that aims at the fubjugation of opinions, and the expulfion of Liberty from the very bofoms of its votaries.

Let our Governors only reconcile themfelves to thefe neceffary conceffions, without which the duration of the war appears to be indefinite, and there remains but one more ftruggle for their pride, the acknowledgment of the French Republic. I appeal to the difpaffionate judgment of my countrymen: can they, by any known rule of juftice, according to any current fyftem of policy, refufe fuch an acknowledgment? Is not France, like England, one of the fovereign, independent ftates of Europe? Have we ever been contented, that foreign potentates fhould queftion our fufficiency to legiflate for ourfelves, or fhould innovate our particular forms of government under colour of general benefit? In the laft century, the people of England deviated at pleafure from a monarchical to a republican eftablifhment, and reverted from republicanifm to monarchy, as the temper of the times varied, indifferent to the approbation or cenfure of their contemporaries.

poraries.* The French claim only that
licence, which the Englifh have ever enjoyed :
what is there fo unreafonable in fuch a claim ?

The Papal hierarchy of Rome had for ages
exercifed jurifdiction over the confciences of
our anceftors: as the power of truth began to
operate, ·and men's minds became enlightened
and enlarged, our forefathers revolted at the
unnatural fubjection, and afferted the rights of
nature. The Holy Church was vehemently
incenfed againft the authors of this impious
rebellion: it vomited forth its anathemas of
damnation, and inftigated the fuperftitious
prejudices of its adherents againft a people,
whofe principles and practice menaced the very
exiftence of the. Catholic religion. But the
fpirit of Englifhmen withftood the attacks of

* "As they had not intermeddled, nor did not intend to
intermeddle, with the affairs of government of any other
kingdom or ftate, fo they did expect the like fair and equal
dealing from abroad, and that they who were not concerned
would not interpofe in the affairs of England ; but in cafe of
fuch an injury, they doubted not, by the courage and power
of the Englifh nation, and the good blefling of God, that they
fhould be fufficiently enabled to make a full defence, and
maintain their own rights." Declaration of the Long Parliament. Macaulay's Hiftory of England, vol. v. chap. ii.

Papal

Papal commination, and perfevered to victory in thofe novel doctrines, fo dreadfully denounced as repugnant againft the temporal welfare, and deftructive to the eternal falvation, of their profeffors. The French are now contending for civil, as we heretofore for religious liberty : and have we the audacity to arreft them in their progrefs, to whom we have marked out the track they fhould purfue ? Let us not fo far condemn our own exertions in former times, and hazard the fecurity of our hard-earned acquifitions, as to join the phalanx of arbitrary princes, to the extinction of liberty and the violation of independence.

Should we once concur in the eftablifhment of a precedent, by which the internal arrangements of individual ftates are rendered amenable to the regulation of a general confederacy, how foon may our prefent conduct be converted into the inftrument of our own deftruction ! The Powers of Europe, fanctioned in their proceedings by our co-operation in the cafe of France, may hereafter difpute the fupremacy of the Britifh Legiflature, and denounce the popular branch of our Conftitution, as inimical to their plans of focial fubordination. Then fhall we be fenfible, when it is

3

too late, that in all attempts for the promotion
of injuſtice, victory is worſe than defeat, and
the attainment of our object deſtined to be
the puniſhment of our aggreſſion. Modifications and limitations of monarchy are fearfully
obnoxious to the pride of arbitrary power: in
a congreſs of Continental Deſpots, the very
ſhadow of a free repreſentation would be
proteſted againſt with every expreſſion of abhorrence: and what a bleſſed code of laws
would Great-Britain receive from the hands of
Pruſſia, Spain, Ruſſia, and the Dii Minorum
Gentium, the petty Princes of the German
Empire!

This laſt, if there were no other, would be
a ſufficient reaſon for our feceſſion from the
league of commiſſioned plunderers and ruffians; for our diſbanding thoſe legions of hunted
Emigrants, whom we are alluring from their
lurking places with the inſidious bait of reſti-
tution; and for adopting that moſt excellent
of all moral maxims, to meaſure our conceſſions to others by our expectations for ourſelves:
in other words, for our acknowledging without
delay the inviolability of the French government, as we would that our own ſhould on a
future day be acknowledged. Let reaſon but

thus

thus far triumph over prejudice, and all other
obftacles in the way of reconciliation will be
eafily furmounted: then may the diabolical
idea of natural antipathy be effaced from the
philofophized minds of both nations, and a
lafting alliance be projected and eftablifhed on
the bafis of reciprocal interefts and confenta-
neous virtues.

The fubftance then and the defign of the
foregoing pages, is to repeat what has fo often
been ineffectually urged, but cannot be too
frequently or too earneftly refubmitted to the
confideration of the public; that the prefent
is an important crifis, in which mifconduct or
error may be of the moft fatal confequence; in
which temerity and fecurity are the forerunners
of certain calamity; to fuggeft to all who have
any voice in the direction of public concerns,
that the nation is anxioufly expecting the fpeedy
return of peace; that the account to which
thofe may be called, who facrifice principle
and a fenfe of general good to private ambition
and the retention of lucrative offices, will
probably be fevere; and above every thing to
recommend with all deference to higher
powers, if they wifh to be greeted with the
acclamations of gratitude through life, and to
tranfmit

tranſmit their names to ſucceding ages with honourable celebrity, to heal the deadly wounds which the beſt intereſts of ſociety are daily receiving from the hand of violence; to withdraw their ſlaughtering legions from an occupation ſo diſgraceful to humanity; and, acting upon principles of true glory and laudable ambition, acknowledging the univerſal rights of man, and the juſt independence of ſeparate communities, to arreſt the preſent progreſs, and as far as in them lies, provide againſt the future revival of ſuch unnatural and uncivilized atrocities : theſe things I would recommend to them, as they would avoid remorſe of conſcience, and the indignation of their ſpecies.

APPENDIX.

I Shall now devote a few pages to the notice of circumſtances, the introduction of which in the preceding chapters would have interrupted the courſe of the argument, and which, though relevant, were not neceſſary to the eſtabliſhment of my poſitions.

I have ſaid in the firſt chapter, that the tax on paper and on Attornies appeared to me objectionable, though I thought it unneceſſary in that place to infiſt on my objections. I will here mention the reaſons for which I diſapprove thoſe taxes : that on paper in particular I conſider as one of the moſt obnoxious, which has been impoſed for many years. It operates as a check on the progreſs of information ; as a burden on a claſs of men, who ought to receive all poſſible encouragement from the ſtate ; thoſe who devote themſelves

felves to literary retirement, and moft effectually contribute to the public welfare, by
the acquifition and diffufion of ufeful knowledge ; but who are diftinguifhed by the trea-
fures of the mind, rather than the fulnefs of
the purfe. It may be confidered as a concealed attack on the Liberty of the Prefs, and
a fumptuary law againft the inftruction of
thofe, to whom inftruction is moft neceffary.
That thefe were the views which materially
contributed to its adoption, will appear from
obferving, that the onus falls on the inferior
forts of paper, which are ufed in printing in
general, and particularly in the printing of
cheap books : while the paper of fuperior
texture, on which the Ariftocracy, efpecially
the female Ariftocracy, delight to fcribble their
elegant nothings, and reiterate profeffions of
unmeaning friendfhip in their truly invaluable
correfpondence, bears but a very inconfiderable
proportion of the general preffure. It is this
principle of taxation, as I have before hinted,
againft the injuftice of which I am fo thoroughly
indignant : and I muft declare, notwithftanding
the general inveteracy againft the French, that
they apportion the burdens to the capacities of
the bearers with a degree of judgment and
equity, of which our Legiflature falls infinitely
                                          fhort.

fhort. I hope the time will come, when every man will be taxed in proportion to his poffeffions; when an income of a thoufand a year will contribute ten times as much towards the exigencies of the ftate, as an income of a hundred a year; in this confifts the rational doctrine of equality.

With regard to the tax on Attornies, I difapprove the principle, though I do not know that it will produce any pernicious effects: it is calculated to convert the profeffion into an Ariftocracy, and eftablifh opulence as the criterion of merit. As to the ground on which it has been fo much applauded, the exclufion of difreputable practitioners, the Chancellor of the Exchequer acknowledged to the Houfe, that it was incompetent to attain fo defirable an end, and that that reptile race would be able to elude all purfuit directed to their annihilation.

———————

In examining the caufes which gave birth to the French Revolution, I have in the fecond chapter traced the effects, which the writings of philofophers and literati gradually produced,

T   from

from the age of Louis the XIVth, to the clofe
of the ancient Monarchy. I have attributed
the alteration of public fentiment to the lef-
fons of thofe Mafters : but there were many
other circumftances contributory to the ac-
celeration of that important event, of which I
omitted the mention, that I might haften to
the main object of the Chapter, the prefent
condition and refources of France. I will here
notice two or three of thofe circumftances.

The foundation of the new edifice was laid
in that fpirit of philofophical inveftigation,
which had gone forth among perfons of condition, and gradually extended its influence
under the aufpices of Royalty: but it would
probably have been long, before the mental
revolution would have difplayed itfelf in overt
acts, had not the united imprudence and profligacy of the Court, the jealoufy of the Ariftocracy, and the derangement of the Finances
at once combined to fhake the pillars of Defpotifm, and reftore to the body of the people
their natural preponderance in the fcale. When
it became neceffary to refort to the convo-
cation of the States General; when an oppofition of intereft arofe between the King
and the Nobility, each party vied with the
other

other in giving confequence to the Tiers-Etat, and reinftating them in their violated rights.

The American war was a powerful means of forwarding the crifis of the Revolution. The exorbitant expences, in which that conteft had involved France as well as England, reduced the government to thofe neceffitous circumftances, which the Ariftocracy had not the virtue to remedy, by a timely facrifice of fuperfluities : which therefore could only be remedied, by extorting from the Peafantry the very fuftenance of life, and fettling the variable opinions of the people into rooted averfion. Nor was this the only method in which the American influenced the French Revolution. To the impolitic conduct of the Queen's party, in enlifting the flaves of defpotifm under the banner of liberty, is principally to be attributed the fubfequent overthrow of Monarchy, and the individual fufferings of the Royal Family. The Queen's defire of humiliating the pride of England, induced her to combat with her influence the reluctance of her Confort; and extort an unwilling acquiefcence in a meafure, of which he feemed to forefee the deftructive confequence. And what was the refult? The

Officers

Officers and Soldiers entered into the merits
of the caufe, for which they were fighting;
caught the fpirit of enthufiafm, fo congenial
to their natures, and fludied the conduct of
their Allies as a model for their own imita-
tion. Nor did a familiar acquaintance with
the characters of Franklin and Wafhington
contribute in a fmall degree, to ftrengthen the
fentiments of patriotifm in the bofoms of
Frenchmen : while the political writings of
Price, fo obnoxious to the fatellites of power,
fo animating to the champions of freedom,
taught France as well as America to unite
zeal with rationality, and inftructed mankind
in the connexion between the duties and the
rights of human nature. The combination of
the provinces of the Netherlands againft the
unjuft violence of Philip of Spain, and the
confequent emancipation of thofe countries,
was an animating precedent in favour of the
Americans in their ftruggle : the event was
fimilar in both inftances : and the hiftory of
the two contefts prefents fo brilliant a fpec-
tacle to the view of France, as will encourage
her to perfevere in the race which fhe has
begun, and by efforts of fuperior power to attain at leaft equal advantages. Thus does the
example of one Revolution invariably contribute

bute towards the eſtabliſhment of another, and facilitate the operations by which it is to be perfeᏨed.

The principal objeᏨion to an immediate peace, as has been ſtated in the fourth Chapter, ariſes from the inſtability of the preſent Government in France, and he infamous characters of the preſent leaders. I have endeavoured to expoſe the fallacy of this objeᏨion; and to ſhew that, whenever a diſpoſition to treat appears in this country, it will be found that the poſſeſſion of the Executive Authority is the only qualification, requiſite to render any party fit perſons, with whom to negotiate. But to ſhew that the preſent rulers in France are not ſo unacquainted with the obligations of duty, as they are repreſented; on the contrary that their ideas riſe to an enviable ſublimity, I ſhall tranſcribe a paſſage from the " Report of the Committee of Public Safety, on the internal policy of the Country, by Maximilian Roberſpierre," which I conſider as unrivalled in its kind: it contains a complete ſyſtem of morality; and if the French nation really aᏨ up to their profeſſion, the continuance

tinuance of hoftilities againft them will be recorded as an aggreffion againft the interefts of humanity, which will reflect lafting difgrace on thofe powers, who remain obftinately implacable againft Republican virtue. "Amongft us we wifh to fubftitute Morality for Egotifm; Probity for Honour; Principles for Cuftoms; Duties for Politeffe; the Empire of Reafon for the Tyranny of Fafhion; contempt of Vice for contempt of Misfortune; Noblenefs for Infolence; Magnanimity for Vanity; the love of Glory for the love of Money; the enjoyment of Happinefs for the ennui of Voluptuoufnefs; the Dignity of the Man for the degeneracy of the Noble; a great, powerful and happy People, for a trifling, frivolous and miferable People; that is, all the Virtues, all the energies of a Republic, for all the Vices and all the Follies of Monarchy.

"We wifh in fhort, to accomplifh the ends of Humanity; to fulfil the promifes of Philofophy; to deftroy the reign of Tyranny and of Crimes; that France, formerly illuftrious only amongft Nations of Slaves, may, by eclipfing the glory of every free People who have ever exifted, become a model for other Nations;

Nations; a terror to Oppreſſors; the conſolation of the Oppreſſed; the ornament of the Univerſe; and that, by cementing our work with our blood, we may at length behold the day-ſtar of univerſal liberty. This is our ambition, this our only aim."

FINIS.

THREE REPORTS of the SELECT COM-MITTEE appointed by the Court of Directors to take into Confideration the Export Trade from Great-Britain to the Eaft-Indies, China, Japan, and Perfia, laid before the Lords' Committee of Privy-Council, with the Appendixes, &c. &c. Price Three Shillings.

" Thefe Reports, which are very interefting, the Publifher has detailed from his PARLIAMENTARY JOURNAL. An Analyfis of Reports of fo multifarious a kind we fhall not attempt, but fhall refer the reader, who wifhes for complete and genuine information, to the Pamphlet itfelf."
Vide Critical Review for July.

" Much valuable and curious information, refpecting the various departments of Eaftern Trade, is comprifed in this Pamphlet. On perufing thefe Three Reports, which are certainly entitled to full credit, one inference is naturally impreifed on the mind of the reader, that the Company's Trade is regulated on more found and fteady principles, than are likely to actuate the loofe, capricious competition of individuals. More truth is to be collected from the prefent ferious inveftigations, than from any occafional party writings." Vide Monthly Review for July.

An ANSWER to Three Scurrilous Pamphlets, entitled, The JOCKEY CLUB. By a MEMBER of the JOCKEY CLUB. Third Edition, Price Two Shillings and Sixpence.

Qui ea quæ vult dicit, ea quæ non vult audiet. TERENCE.

ANECDOTES of the LIFE of the Right Honourable WILLIAM PITT, EARL of CHATHAM, and of the principal Events of his Time, with his Speeches in Parliament from the Year 1736 to the Year 1778. Third Edition, corrected, in three Volumes, Price Eighteen Shillings in Boards.

NEW PUBLICATIONS,

Printed for J. S. JORDAN, No. 166, Fleet-Street.

A COMPLETE COLLECTION of STATE PAPERS,

FOR THE YEAR 1793.

This Day was Published, Price 9s. Half Bound;

Containing an accurate and particular Account of all the Military Operations in Flanders, on the Rhine, in Vendée, at Toulon; the Letters of Sir James Murray, General O'Hara, Lord Hood, Lord Mulgrave, Lord Yarmouth, of the French Commissioners at Lyons, Strasburgh, and with the several Armies; all the Accounts in the London Gazette, and by the French Convention. Together with all the important State Papers, Manifestoes, and Memorials of England, France, Prussia, Germany, Switzerland, Genoa, Tuscany, States General, Naples, Austria, French Princes, Sweden, Denmark, Russia, Poland, and America, from the Year 1791 to the present Time. There is no other complete Collection of these Authentic Documents in the English Language:

The FIFTH VOLUME of

THE POLITICAL STATE OF EUROPE.

THIS Work (which is published in Monthly Numbers, Price One Shilling each, and will be continued to the End of the War) contains such a Series of important Papers as are not to be met with in any other Publication whatever. And these, being elucidated by the Official Detail of all public Events, render it not only the most useful, but the most impartial, History of the present Times. Here every Reader is perfectly enabled to judge for himself, from having the true Accounts of both Sides constantly laid before him.

Complete Sets may be had in Numbers, Price 1l. 15s. Or the five first Volumes, to the End of the Year 1793, half bound in Russia, Price Two Guineas.

While the Peace of Nations is rent by contending Parties at Home and Abroad, how interesting and intelligent it must be to those, who are searching for Truth, unbiassed by Faction, to find such an impartial Statement of Facts and Occurrences, from all Parties, Sects, and Nations, as are and will be truly collected in this Work, during a Conflict, in which the whole World daily becomes more and more interested.

As a Testimony of our Impartiality, the Editors will thankfully receive every Hint of Improvement, that can be suggested by any Party; Truth, disinterested Truth, being the most essential Ground of our Plan.

PARLIAMENTARY REPORTS.

THE ONLY VOLUME PUBLISHED OF

PARLIAMENTARY DEBATES to the PRESENT TIME:

Containing the important Debates at Length, in both Houfes, on landing Foreign Troops in this Kingdom—all the Debates on the late Treaties with Foreign Powers, and authentic Copies of all thofe Treaties. Debates on augmenting the Militia—on the Slave-Trade—on the Attornies Tax Bill—on the Indemnity Bill—on the Cafes of Muir and Palmer—on the Scotch Law—on the Mutiny Bill—on Want of Convoys—on the State of Nova Scotia—the Earl of Moira's Explanation of his Conduct—Marquis of Lanfdown's Motion for Peace—on the Budget—Augmentation of the Army—on the Navy—on the Seizure of French Property—Earl of Stanhope's Motion to acknowledge the French Republic—on the Captures made by the French—on exorbitant Salaries—on the King's Speech, and on the Addreffes in both Houfes. Alfo the Debates on a great Number of other Subjects, the Lift of which is too long for an Advertifement. Together with all the Protefts—the feveral Accounts of the Revenue—the Lifts of the Divifions—and all other Papers laid before Parliament.

This Day is Publifhed,

The FIRST VOLUME of

JORDAN's PARLIAMENTARY JOURNAL,

OF THE PRESENT SESSION,

Price Six Shillings in Boards.

THIS Work contains a faithful Detail of all the Debates and Proceedings of both Houfes of Parliament; which, in the prefent Situation of Public Affairs, is interefting to Perfons of all Ranks. It is publifhed Weekly, in Numbers, Price only Sixpence each. Number XV. containing the Preliminary Articles between Great-Britain and Hanover, relative to his Majefty's Hanoverian Forces, which are to be taken into the Pay of Great-Britain, was publifhed this Day; and Number XVII. will be publifhed next Saturday; and will go on regularly every Week to the End of the Seffion.

The JOURNAL of the LAST SESSION may be had in Three Volumes, Price Eighteen Shillings in Boards, or One Guinea, Half Bound in Ruffia; being the ONLY Work that contains the EAST-INDIA REPORTS, &c. &c.

NEW PUBLICATIONS,
Printed for J. S. JORDAN, No. 1,6, Fleet-Street.

BRISSOT.

NEW TRAVELS IN THE UNITED STATES OF AMERICA, performed in 1788; containing the latest and moft accurate Obfervations on the Character, Genius, and prefent State of the People and Government of that Country: their Agriculture, Commerce, Manufactures, and Finances; Quality and Price of Lands, and Progrefs of the Settlements on the Ohio and the Miffiffippi; political and moral Character of the Quakers, and a Vindication of that excellent Sect, from the Mifreprefentations of other Travellers; State of the Blacks; Progrefs of the Laws for their Emancipation, and for the fina Deftruction of Slavery on that Continent: accurate Accounts of the Climate, Longevity; comparative Tables of the Probabilities of Life between America and Europe, &c. &c. By J. P. BRISSOT DE WARVILLE. Second Edition, corrected, Price Six Shillings in Boards.

** The very favourable Reception which the firft Edition of this Volume has met with, demands the warmeft Acknowledgements of the Editor. This Indulgence has encouraged him to collect from BRISSOT's other Papers, a Second Volume upon the fame Subject; to which will be added, feveral original Papers, illuftrative of the fame; the whole containing a Series of Information, not lefs interefting to every Britifh Reader. It is now in the Prefs, and will fpeedily be publifhed, with a Portrait of the Author, finely engraved, from a Print lately publifhed at Paris.

OBSERVATIONS on the PASSAGE between the ATLANTIC and PACIFIC OCEANS, in two MEMOIRS of the Straits of Anian, and the Difcoveries of De Fonte, elucidated by a new and original Map; to which is prefixed an Hiftorical Abridgement of Difcoveries in the NORTH of AMERICA. Infcribed to the Merchants trading to the North-Weft Coaft of America, by William Goldfon, in Quarto, price Eight Shillings in Boards.

CAPTAIN PACKENHAM's Invention of a Subftitute for a LOST RUDDER, and to prevent its being Loft; alfo a Method of reftoring the Mafts of Ships when wounded or otherwife injured, price One Shilling and Sixpence.

A LETTER to a GENTLEMAN of the PHILANTHROPIC SOCIETY, on the LIBERTY OF THE PRESS. By PERCIVAL STOCKDALE. Price Sixpence.

" To check the legal Freedom of the Prefs, is to ftrike at the Root of all our Liberties."

From the LAST PARIS COPY, printed by Authority,
Ornamented with a fine *Portrait* of the late QUEEN of FRANCE,
Efteemed a moft ftriking Likenefs,

The GENUINE TRIAL of the late QUEEN of FRANCE;
containing all the Charges brought againft her by the Public
Accufer; the private Interrogatory of the Queen; and the
Examination of the Witneffes, all at full Length; together
with the Charge of the Prefident to the Jury, and the feveral
Particulars of her Execution. The whole difplaying a Number of Facts concerning, and comprehending a general View
of the Caufes of, the late REVOLUTION IN FRANCE. Second
Edition, corrected, price One Shilling.

*** There are a few Copies printed on fine Wove Paper, Hot Preffed,
with a COLOURED PORTRAIT, price Half-a-Crown.

COMMENTARIES 'on the CONSTITUTION of the
UNITED STATES of AMERICA, to which is prefixed an
authentic Copy of the CONSTITUTION; in which are un-
folded the Principles of free Government, and the fuperior
advantages of Republicanifm demonftrated. By James Wilfon,
L. L. D. Profeffor of Laws in the College and Univerfity of
the Commonwealth of Pennfylvania, one of the Affociate
Judges of the Supreme Court of the United-States, and appointed by the Legiflature of Pennfylvania to form a Digeft of
the Laws of that State; and by Thomas M'Kean, L. L. D.
Chief Juftice of the Commonwealth of Pennfylvania. The
whole extracted from the Debates publifhed in Philadelphia.
By Thomas Lloyd. Price Three Shillings.

The Monthly Review for October, 1792, fays " that the Contents of
this Pamphlet are fully expreffed in the Title: but the Publication muft
be perufed throughout, in order to form an Idea of the good Senfe and
manly Eloquence of the Speeches here made public. The Merits of the
AMERICAN CONSTITUTION, not only generally with refpect to its
Principles on which it is built, but efpecially with regard to its feveral
Objects, are herein well difcuffed."

LAWS CONCERNING PROPERTY IN LITERARY
PRODUCTIONS, in ENGRAVINGS, DESIGNINGS, and
ETCHINGS, ufeful for Authors, Printers, Bookfellers, Engra-
vers, Defigners, and Printfellers. Shewing the Nature and
prefent State of fuch Property, and the Mode of fecuring it.
Price One Shilling and Sixpence.

A DIALOGUE IN THE SHADES, between MERCURY,
a NOBLEMAN, and a MECHANIC. Price One Shilling.

www.ingramcontent.com/pod-product-compliance
Lightning Source LLC
Chambersburg PA
CBHW020558270326
41927CB00006B/893